HOW PLAYS
ARE MADE

D1039185

Donated By

Property of
CUAdrama

Donnell De

Stuart Griffiths

HOW PLAYS ARE MADE

THE FUNDAMENTAL ELEMENTS OF PLAY CONSTRUCTION

A SPECTRUM BOOK

Prentice-Hall, Inc., Englewood Cliffs, New Jersey 07632

Library of Congress Cataloging in Publication Data

Griffiths, Stuart.
    How plays are made.

    "A Spectrum Book."
    Bibliography: p.
    Includes index.
    1. Drama—Technique.   2. Playwriting.   I. Title.
PN1661.G72 1984   808.2   83-24474
ISBN 0-13-428145-4
ISBN 0-13-428137-3 (pbk.)

© 1982 by Stuart Griffiths. First published in Great Britain by Heinemann
Educational Books Ltd., 22 Bedford Square, London WC1B 3HH.
Revised American edition © 1984 by Prentice-Hall, Inc., Englewood Cliffs,
New Jersey 07632.
All rights reserved. No part of this book may be reproduced in any form
or by any means without permission in writing from the publisher.
A Spectrum Book. Printed in the United States of America.

10 9 8 7 6 5 4 3 2 1

ISBN 0-13-428145-4

ISBN 0-13-428137-3 {PBK.}

Editorial/production supervision by Elizabeth Torjussen
Cover design by Hal Siegel
Manufacturing buyer: Edward J. Ellis

This book is available at a special discount when ordered in
bulk quantities. Contact Prentice-Hall, Inc., General
Publishing Division, Special Sales, Englewood Cliffs, N.J. 07632.

Prentice-Hall International, Inc., *London*
Prentice-Hall of Australia Pty. Limited, *Sydney*
Prentice-Hall Canada Inc., *Toronto*
Prentice-Hall of India Private Limited, *New Delhi*
Prentice-Hall of Japan, Inc., *Tokyo*
Prentice-Hall of Southeast Asia Pte. Ltd., *Singapore*
Whitehall Books Limited, *Wellington, New Zealand*
Editora Prentice-Hall do Brasil Ltda., *Rio de Janeiro*

CONTENTS

For my parents

FOREWORD

by Keith Williams
Head of Plays, BBC Television Drama
January 1984

This new American edition brings *How Plays Are Made* to a wider public, one which has traditionally paid special attention to dramatic technique. The content is unchanged, and the note format remains. Practicing playwrights and students in North America should find this concentrated presentation of material particularly useful.

The book is an expansion of a set of notes on play construction Stuart Griffiths originally wrote for writers when he joined BBC Television. Since 1977, he has been the script editor of Classic Plays, the television equivalent of a theater *Dramaturg* or literary manager. He has also been much involved in advising and guiding writers.

The question is frequently asked, "What exactly is meant by play construction?" There can be no simple answer any more than there can be immutable rules in any art form. It embraces those fundamental principles of the writer's craft that have been established through practice across the centuries.

Rigidity in applying the principles would, of course, inhibit imaginative innovation. The purpose of this book however is quite simply to examine and describe the fundamental elements of the craft. Without this knowledge, any writer is surely at a disadvantage. It is also intended for the general reader who wishes to know more about the inner workings of drama.

My thanks are due to the following authors and publishers for the inclusion of brief extracts from their named works.

The executors of George Pierce Baker; Houghton, Mifflin, Co., Boston, and Greenwood Press: *Dramatic Technique*. The executors of Percival Wilde; Little, Brown and Co., Boston, The Writer Inc., Boston, and Jonathan Cape Ltd.: *The Craftsmanship of the One-Act Play*. Dover Publications Inc., New York: William Archer's *Play-Making*. Walter Kerr and The Writer Inc., Boston: *How Not to Write a Play*. Eric Bentley and Methuen Ltd.: *The Life of the Drama*. Arthur Miller, The Viking Press, New York and Secker and Warburg Ltd.: *The Crucible, Death of a Salesman*, and the introduction to the collected plays. The executors of Edith Sitwell, and Macmillan Ltd.: *A Notebook on William Shakespeare*. The Society of Authors and the Shaw estate: *You Never Can Tell, Arms and the Man, Major Barbara, Our Theatres in the Nineties*. The Harley Granville Barker estate, the Society of Authors, and Sidgwick and Jackson Ltd.: *Waste*. The Sean O'Casey estate and Macmillan Ltd.: *Juno and the Paycock*. The Eugene O'Neill estate and Jonathan Cape Ltd.: *Mourning Becomes Electra*. The G. K. Chesterton estate and J. M. Dent & Co.: the introduction to *Pickwick Papers*.

The Noel Coward estate and Heinemann Ltd.: *Hay Fever, Private Lives*. Samuel Beckett and Faber and Faber Ltd.: *All That Fall*. John Osborne and Faber and Faber Ltd.: *Time Present*. Harold Pinter and Eyre Methuen Ltd.: *The Caretaker, A Slight Ache*, and *No Man's Land*. Harold Pinter, Aidan Higgins, Calder and Boyars Ltd., the BBC, and Max Rosenberg: *Langrishe, Go Down*. My thanks also to Harold Pinter for permission to quote from his rehearsal instructions to the cast of the BBC Television production of *The Hothouse*. Edward Albee, Atheneum, New York, and Jonathan Cape Ltd.: *Who's Afraid of Virginia Woolf?* Tom Stoppard and Faber and Faber Ltd.: *The Real*

Inspector Hound, Rosencrantz and Guildenstern are Dead. Edward
Bond, Eyre Methuen Ltd. and the Royal Court Theater: *Restoration.*
Sir John Gielgud and Heinemann Ltd.: *Stage Directions.* Don Shaw
and the BBC: *Wingate Trilogy.* Eugène Ionesco, Donald Watson
(translator) and John Calder Ltd.: *Victims of Duty.* Lorrimer
Publishing Ltd. and Universal City Studios Inc.: *Monkey Business.*

E. F. Watling and Penguin Books Ltd. for translations from
Oedipus Rex and *Antigone.* Ronald Hingley and the Oxford Uni-
versity Press for translations from *Uncle Vanya* and *The Seagull.*
Michael Meyer and Rupert Hart-Davis Ltd. for translations from
Rosmersholm and *Hedda Gabler.* The executors of Constance
Garnett, and Heinemann Ltd. for translations from *Crime and
Punishment* and *Anna Karenina.* The executors of A. G. Chater,
Charles Scribner's Sons, and Da Capo Press, New York: *From Ibsen's
Workshop.* The E. M. Forster estate, Edward Arnold Ltd. and
Penguin Books Ltd.: *Aspects of the Novel.* John Willett, the Brecht
estate, and Methuen Ltd.: *Brecht on Theatre.*

The executors of George Kaufman and Moss Hart; and Random
House, New York: *The Man Who Came to Dinner.* The H. G. Wells
estate, Howard Koch, Orson Welles, CBS, and Manheim Fox Enter-
prises, Inc.: *The War of the Worlds.* Herman J. Mankiewicz's execu-
tors, Orson Welles, RKO Radio Pictures, Bantam Books Ltd.: *Citizen
Kane.* The executors of Moss Hart, and Secker and Warburg Ltd.: *Act
One.* Dover Publications Inc., New York: *Hamburg Dramaturgy.* Ben
Hecht and David Selznick's executors, Viking Press, and Macmillan
Ltd.: *Memo from David O. Selznick.* Alfred Hitchcock's executors,
François Truffaut, and Granada Publishing Ltd.: *Hitchcock.* Dorothy
Parker's executors, and Penguin Books Ltd. The executors of T. S. Eliot
and Cyril Connolly, and Hamish Hamilton Ltd.: *The Unquiet Grave.*
Gore Vidal, the executors of Kenneth Tynan, and *The Observer.* The
Dashiell Hammett estate, John Huston, and Warner Brothers Pictures
Inc.: *The Maltese Falcon.* The executors of Howard Lindsay. The Max
Beerbohm estate and Rupert Hart-Davis Ltd.: *Around Theatres.* Jules
Feiffer and Penguin Books Ltd. The James Joyce estate, The Bodley
Head, and Random House: *Ulysses.*

To the BBC for the quotation from my adaptation of the text of
Danton's Death. The description of Olivier's Othello and the parody
of *Long Day's Journey into Night* were adapted from articles that I
wrote in the London *Evening Standard.*

INTRODUCTION

1

*It was. . .an excellent play, well digested in the scenes, set down
with as much modesty as cunning.*

The word 'playwright' is accurate for anyone who practices play
making. He is a maker of plays, as a shipwright is a builder of
ships. The construction of a play is a difficult and specialized craft,
but it can be learned.

Craft alone does not, of course, equip someone to write good
plays—any more than an architect or a carpenter who has completed his training or apprenticeship can then build a Wren church
or make a Sheraton chair.

No one can teach an aspiring playwright how to create living,
breathing characters who deeply engage an audience's sympathies.
No one can teach him to write vital dialogue charged with tension
and humor. But, if the talent is there, knowing early how a play is
constructed can save years of trial and error. It can accelerate a
writer's growth and enable him to find his voice much sooner. It
can save many a budding talent from extinction through
discouragement.

Baker's Course

In the early years of this century, Eugene O'Neill and several other students who subsequently won acclaim on Broadway attended Professor George Pierce Baker's two-year play-writing course at Harvard. Their debt to him was considerable. Baker did not create O'Neill's genius, but he nurtured it, guided it, accelerated its development. His other students included Sidney Howard, Robert Sherwood, Philip Barry, and S. N. Behrman. Baker's lectures have been published under the title *Dramatic Technique*. They are worth careful study.

R. C. Sherriff pays tribute in his autobiography to William Archer's *Play-Making*, the other central treatise on the craft of play construction. Sherriff had a rich store of experience and creative emotion to realize in dramatic form. The book was clearly important in shaping it effectively and bringing his famous war play, *Journey's End*, into being.

Noel Coward acknowledged his debt to Somerset Maugham, who urged the vital importance of good construction in comedy. Apart from their other qualities, Coward's best comedies—*Hay Fever*, *Private Lives*, *Blithe Spirit*—are brilliantly constructed. He could "write dialogue by the yard," but his whole approach to play writing was that no amount of marvelous interior decorating would avail if the foundations of the house were no good.

Well-Made Plays

Coward, Sherriff, and Maugham were, of course, masters of the "well-made play." This has become a pejorative term, mainly associated with the highly artificial nineteenth-century product. But the truly well-made play is so enthralling, audiences are never aware how well constructed it is. The internal mechanism does not show. They cannot see the wheels going around. No one describes Beckett's *All That Fall* or Pinter's *The Homecoming* as well-made plays in the accepted sense. But they are, in fact, supremely well made.

Holding Attention

A playwright's first duty is to keep his audiences awake: to hook, retain, and intensify their interest. Unless he holds their attention, the play fails. In fact, play construction is simply a body of knowledge gathered over the centuries from the observation of audience reaction.

All plays that survive from any period and outlast fashion fall back on first principles. These basic principles apply to any form of drama—theater, film, television, radio. They often exist in other literary and artistic forms, which is why examples from novels have been included in this book.

Long Tradition

What appears new will on closer inspection be revealed as part of a familiar dramatic tradition. Films for example have influenced modern playwrights with their swift movement, loose episodic structure, sudden cuts, compression, and economy. But the Shakespearean structure is also cinematic. The same applies to the works of Brecht and to Georg Büchner's *Woyzeck*. These have had a considerable impact on English playwrights today, such as Edward Bond, John Arden, David Hare, and Howard Brenton.

Woyzeck, a play written in 1836 that had an important influence on Brecht, is structurally like the script of a new play, film, or television drama of the 1980s. Of his own mentors, Büchner wrote that two authors mattered: Shakespeare and (occasionally) Goethe. "The rest you can throw on the fire."

The work of leading American dramatists is rooted in dramatic tradition. The influence of Ibsen on the plays of Arthur Miller is profound. Tennessee Williams was strongly influenced by Strindberg and Chekhov, as is Edward Albee by Strindberg and Eliot. Eugene O'Neill was dominated by the Greeks. These influences are not just of themes or ideas; they are structural.

The most original playwrights will often admit later their indebtedness to models who have been around a very long time. Shaw, who astonished his early audiences, later acknowledged that his work owed a great deal to Sophocles, Aristophanes, Molière, and Shakespeare.

This book is about the first principles of drama. It is primarily intended to help new writers, but it is hoped it will also be useful to the general reader who wishes to understand more about the technique of play writing.

4

A good starting point is to ask what sinks a play. The most common charges leveled by an audience against a bad play are that it is slow, boring, or implausible. This corresponds to the absence of the three essential elements in drama: action, tension, and characters that live.

ACTION

2

Action is drama's most mysterious element. Formidable thinkers on the subject throughout history concur that it is also the most important. Indeed, drama *is* action. The word itself is derived from the ancient Greek word "to do." Lessing rightly said that all practitioners of the art and all critics must return to the plumb-line of Aristotle's writings on the drama. Those utterances are oracular and appropriately cryptic at times. Aristotle defined tragedy as "an imitation of the Action" and left it to posterity to work out exactly what he meant.

One interpretation could be that the process of a drama, the whole curve of its action, should parallel some fundamental rhythm or movement of nature. The action of a good play has often been compared to a wave making toward the seashore: small at first, swelling higher and higher, with a steady rising and falling movement, at its highest peak breaking and crashing on the shore, then the sudden final falling away. Breathing; a beating heart; the cycle of the seasons; of a human life; the course of a single day; the act of coitus: they are all valid comparisons. In another art form, the process can be realized in a great symphony.

First Thoughts

The action of a good play may be sensed by its author before the plot detail, characters, or dialogue. The writer may have a vague yet insistent general idea of what the play should be, and its action grows from that.

The rising action, the climactic action, combined possibly with a reversal, where the action veers around to its opposite, then the falling action and resolution, will be mapped out before a word of a play is written. In fact, the actual writing is a minor part of the work for many dramatists. It is done very rapidly. The play may have been gestating for months or even years beforehand. In different ways Ibsen, Noel Coward, Arthur Miller, John Osborne, Harold Pinter, Tom Stoppard and Alan Ayckbourn have all testified to this creative phenomenon.

Similar experiences are to be found in other artistic areas. Chesterton wrote of Dickens' first masterpiece: "A man knows the style of the book he wants to write when he knows nothing else about it. The idea of light existed when there was not a single solitary star. Pickwick is the mere mass of light before the creation of the sun or moon."

Change: *Othello*

When one talks of a play's "action," it is not physical action. That is only part of the process. Action must never be confused with mere activity or bustle. A drama can have a great action that carries an audience with it from beginning to end with hardly one burst of physical violence. Emotional and mental action are what count.

The long temptation scene in *Othello* (Act III, Scene 3) consists mainly of two men talking together. The physical action is minimal. Yet the mental stress and emotional violence of the scene are tremendous. Before our eyes we see a terrible change taking place. As we watch, Othello gradually changes, through Iago's poison, from a state of calm noble stability into one of mad, uncontrollable fury and jealousy. The Moor changes, as it were, from black to green to red.

If that scene had been left out, and Desdemona simply

reported to Emilia that her husband had undergone an awful transformation, the audience would have felt cheated. They actually want to see the transformation taking place.

Opposed Forces

Equally important for dramatic action is the opposition of evenly matched forces. If one force has its way too easily from start to finish, the audience will lose interest. If it is met by an opposition worthy of it, the contending forces strain against each other and sway this way or that according to whichever has the advantage; there is stress, tension, struggle, and a seesaw of fortunes until the issue is resolved. It may be a conflict of individual wills, of ideas, of moral choices, of a man's purpose with some obstruction or flaw in his own nature. Eric Bentley, the noted theater scholar, has compared a dramatist to a perverse traffic policeman. Instead of keeping the traffic from hitting each other, he beckons and guides them into collision.

Goals and Obstacles

The need for conflict in drama can be misunderstood. It is generally better for the dramatist to concentrate on the idea of a man striving to achieve a goal and meeting resistance from an obstacle or succession of obstacles. The goal may change, of course. (Coriolanus first intends to rule Rome, then to destroy it.) But it is hard to think of any great play where the principle does not apply. The obstructed will is the closest one can get to a universal dramatic theme.

The obstruction need not be external, for example a villain. Hamlet, Coriolanus, and Macbeth are examples of a protagonist whose purpose is frustrated and finally doomed by obstacles within his own nature.

Furthermore, the Shakespearean action is often marked by a striking reversal after the half-way point, as happens in *Julius Caesar*, *Macbeth*, and *Coriolanus*, where the rising movement, carrying the fortunes of the protagonist, is met by a counter-movement, that has nonetheless been built into the ground plan of the action from the start, and that ultimately prevails. This reversal, or revolution, provides the dynamic for the second half of the play.

The Play's Driver

In many plays the central character striving for his or her objective is the one who guns the action forward. But this is not always the case, and someone must be there to do it. There is a toy called Action Man; and in a sense every good play has its action man. At each stage, a play needs a driver, a galvanizer, an activator, a doer, a powerful will, someone who makes things happen. This may be the hero or villain, male or female, (Henry V, Richard III, Lady Macbeth), a supremely competent operator (Mr. Voysey in Granville Barker's *The Voysey Inheritance*), or a perpetrator of comic disasters (Norman in Ayckbourn's *The Norman Conquests* or, in films, M. Hulot or Harpo Marx).

The King is the initial driver of *Hamlet*, and he starts the play long before the curtain rises by killing his brother and marrying Gertrude. Goneril and Edmund are the drivers of *King Lear*, as well as the King himself. Voysey Senior drives the first part of *The Voysey Inheritance*; then his son Edward takes over (see p. 13). These are not passive characters; they thrust the play onward. They have objectives, and they combat resistance. If the play is in danger of running out of steam, a new driver can always be introduced. Powerful and colorful characters can be saved for the last act; Shaw does this with General Burgoyne in *The Devil's Disciple*, and Bohun QC in *You Never Can Tell*.

The Process

Walter Kerr, the writer and Broadway theater critic, has summed up the process of a dramatic action: "There is a beginning stage in any change: a stage at which motivating pressures are beginning to clamor for a response. There is a middle stage: a stage at which the response is given and the inevitable conflict joined. There is an end stage: a stage at which the contest between pressure and response has resulted in a different relationship between these two things, a new state of affairs, a changed state of affairs.... All that is asked of the dramatist is that he show the beginnings of some one particular change, that he trace it through its natural turmoil, and that he bring the contending forces into a different—though not necessarily a perfect—balance. Things were one way; now they are another; we have seen them move."

Examples

Julius Caesar

The pressure clamoring for a response in *Julius Caesar* is Caesar's growing dictatorial power. Sedition is rife, embodied in the fiery Cassius (the driving force), who must first persuade the respected moderate Brutus to lead a conspiracy. This is not so easy—the two wills are matched in strength. Cassius' passion and the fear that Caesar will shortly be crowned king eventually sway Brutus, and others. The conspiracy swiftly gathers momentum, its objective Caesar's murder. The play rises to its formal climax—the assassination—and surpasses that with a great reversal, when Antony's oratory turns the tables on the conspirators and starts the counter-movement of the tragedy that will finally destroy them.

Coriolanus

Coriolanus is the patrician hero of Rome whose objective, in the long central section of the drama, is to become Consul—but not at the cost to his ferocious pride (the internal obstacle) of abasing himself before the plebeian electors. Although he will not show them his battle wounds, the puzzled plebeians consent to his election; but the Tribunes (driving the action forward) persuade them to revoke their decision. Coriolanus (his own fatal enemy) blazes up in rage at the Tribunes. The people turn against him, and there is a riot. The rising fortunes of Coriolanus thus take a sudden downswing on collision with an opposing force.

His strong mother Volumnia cools his passion and urges policy (one mind swayed by another). For the moment, Coriolanus changes. He returns to the Forum, prepared to be more conciliatory. But the Tribunes (pitching the action forward) accuse him of being a tyrant and traitor. At this, all restraint flies from him, and the play soars to its climax. In a towering fury, Coriolanus curses the Tribunes and the people. On the instant they banish him from Rome. He turns his back on the city with terrible finality. It is a majestic reversal, a "peripeteia," soon after the half-way mark, where the drama does a 180-degree about-turn.

Much is still to come—Coriolanus joins forces with the Volscians, his former enemies, and marches on Rome. But in this central span of the tragedy there is turbulent movement, great passion, the

12

collision of mighty opposites, and an incessant, drastic alternation of fortunes. It is a splendid dramatic action.

The Iceman Cometh

Eugene O'Neill's late masterpiece portrays a group of down-and-outs in a New York flop house, living on their pipe dreams. The play's driver, a traveling salesman named Hickey, challenges their illusions, breaks down their resistance, and achieves his objective: He makes the derelicts face the cruel truth about themselves. Hickey himself however has a terrible secret, which the counter-movement of the drama forces him to reveal. The play is very long, but it has a sustained dramatic action, entailing a vehement obstructed will, continually changing states of mind, and deep emotional turmoil.

Galileo

In Brecht's *Life of Galileo*, free rational thought challenges authority and dogmatism. Galileo strives to propagate scientific truth, but is opposed by the Catholic Church which denounces his beliefs as heretical. When Galileo persists in disseminating the new Copernican system, proving that the earth is not the center of the universe, the Church gets tougher: He is summoned before the Inquisition. Eventually he is forced unheroically to recant. (The internal obstacle is his sensual nature and love of comfort.) But the play shows he does not betray science completely.

The Voysey Inheritance

Harley Granville Barker (1877-1946), dramatist, actor, director, and scholar was a contemporary of Shaw and remains a major force in the twentieth-century English theater. His brilliant plays, especially *The Voysey Inheritance* and *Waste*, have an elliptical style on the page, but are hypnotic in performance. He could create superb women characters. Some American readers may find the "Englishness" of the plays initially difficult, but this can quickly be overcome to yield rich rewards.

In Granville Barker's play *The Voysey Inheritance*, the head of a noted firm of solicitors shocks his son Edward, the junior partner, when he calmly tells him he has been swindling his clients for years without detection. He did not begin this; he inherited the corrupt practice from his father before him. Necessity, as well as a buccaneering spirit, has motivated him. In due course Voysey Senior dies, and Edward is left in an appalling dilemma. Most of his family are stunned when he tells them. They favor the path of expediency but really leave the decisions to him. Edward embarks on the laborious and highly risky course of attempting to put right the crooked finances of the firm, living constantly under the threat of discovery and imprisonment. Events in the latter half of the play show how dangerous this course is.

Edward thus comes to terms with his inheritance, and the process involves a fundamental dramatic action. Granville Barker depicts a man's struggle with his destiny, his resolve to strive with an almost intolerable burden and overcome severe obstacles, internal and external. Edward changes, moreover, with the stress and responsibility, from something of a prig and a weakling in the first act, when his first impulse is to confess or leave the firm, to a grown man, worldly yet moral, dealing his own sense of right and wrong at the play's end. He travels a formidable journey. The play, of course, has other remarkable qualities and splendid characters, men and women, but this is its central action.

Causation

E. M. Forster said that a story depends only on time. "The King died, and then the Queen died" is a mere succession of events in time. A plot depends on causation. "The King died, and then the Queen died of grief" is a plot. The principle of causality is essential to drama. It must not be an unrelated succession of incidents or episodes. It may appear so at the beginning—particularly in a fast-moving, sharply edited film, or a radio or television drama that moves rapidly between past and present and from one locale to another. The audience does not knit together the disparate events, the shifts in space and time, until later. But that is simply the delayed emergence of causality.

The action of a good play always points forward. It has a logical chain of cause and effect, with one scene leading on to another, in a sequence that has an organic growth, and that, once the audience's sympathies and passions are engaged, will carry them along in a strong current to the conclusion.

Action and character become indistinguishable. Things happen because a man is what he is and, as the play advances, its events change him. "Character is destiny." The drama moves by its own inner necessity. It is driven finally by its own internal logic.

King Lear

The first scene of *King Lear* rolls aside a boulder that has been holding back an avalanche for many years. It starts a process that will not stop until the last line of the tragedy is reached. Lear divides his kingdom. He disinherits his youngest daughter Cordelia because she refuses to make an excessive public declaration of love for him and banishes the Earl of Kent because he defends her. Given their characters, a clash between Lear and his two eldest daughters, Goneril and Regan, is now inevitable, and it grows logically. Lear would continue to think he could play the King and not restrain the hundred arrogant knights who attend on him. The fatal quarrel's inception is when Goneril tells her servants to treat Lear with less respect. When this occurs, his rage begins to mount.

Crucial stages intensifying the action are Goneril's dismissal of half her father's knights; and, when he turns to Regan, the placing of his messenger (the disguised Kent) in the stocks. At its height, Lear is beset by his two daughters, both competing to reduce the number of his knights. When Regan finally says "What need one?" Lear cracks. Since he cannot now banish them, he banishes himself—into the storm. Madness and beggary follow as a natural consequence. But from this ultimate reduction—absolute monarch to less than a beast ("a dog's obeyed in office")—springs self-knowledge, compassion, and forgiveness.

Danton's Death

Here are some key scenes from Büchner's *Danton's Death* (1835), probably the greatest play about revolution ever written.

Danton, the mighty but disillusioned hero of the French Revolution, disports with prostitutes in a Paris brothel.

Danton clashes with Robespierre, the high priest of the Revolution and architect (with Saint-Just) of the Reign of Terror. Danton's guilt over the September Massacres, for which he was responsible two years earlier, makes him recoil vehemently from a worse blood-bath; and his lustful nature is repelled by Robespierre's frigid puritanism. Robespierre in turn hates him and determines to eliminate him.

Danton tells his fiery young disciples he is sickened by the Revolution and bored with life. He rejects their exhortations to take up the torch of leadership again. He ignores warnings that the Terror needs a redundant hero, "one heavy head." Trusting in his legend, he refuses to escape.

Danton has a terrible nightmare about the September Massacres the night before he is arrested.

These and other scenes clearly set down the milestones to Danton's execution. He fights back heroically at his trial but fails to save himself. He goes to the guillotine because of what he has done and what he is.

Dramatic Action and the Historical Process _____

In performance, *Danton's Death* benefits from some cutting and reshaping. I adapted the play with its director, Alan Clarke, for BBC Television in 1978. In particular, we reduced the metaphysical discussion, fascinating though it is, because it tends toward repetition and impedes forward movement. But the principle of causation nonetheless operates with great force. For Büchner, while telling the story of one colorful figure, is making a profound philosophical statement about the historical process.

The high point is Saint-Just's terrifying speech to the Convention, which uncannily foreshadows Stalin and Hitler in its cold assertion that the slaughter of tens of thousands is necessary for the creation of a New Order, a rebirth for mankind. He is given an ovation, but his triumph is short lived. The tigers of the Revolution have been unleashed. Though it is outside the time span of the play, he and Robespierre will fall victim to their own ideology and follow Danton to the guillotine three months later. Saint-Just's own words are in fact his death warrant: "We call upon tyrannicides of the future who, across Europe, bear under their cloaks the dagger of Brutus—nay, we summon all the secret enemies of Tyranny, throughout the entire earth, to share with us this sublime hour!"

The drama thus depicts a revolution with remorseless logic devouring its own children. Dramatically and historically it has a fatal chain of consequences, an inevitability of cause and effect that is essential to any definition of Action.

Lighting the Fuse

There is a concept of dramaturgy called "the lighting of the fuse," the moment when the play really begins, the entry of an exciting force when the play takes off and rises to its climax. What precedes this moment is the slow assembly of inflammable materials. But it is a hazardous practice, unless the dramatist really knows what he is doing, not to move things along as soon as the curtain rises. Modern audiences are impatient with slow openings. Nor does it accord with dramatic tradition—Shakespeare's best plays start with a bang, and it is very satisfying to be plunged straight into the action.

Climax

When rising tension and emotion culminate in an explosion, a turning point, or simply a moment of high intensity and excitement, this constitutes a climax. A dramatic story is full of climaxes from beginning to end, some necessarily of greater importance than others—often placed at the end of acts.

The major climax of a drama, where the action rises to its highest pitch, is the most intense and turbulent. It is the culminating point of suspense, the point of maximum instability. Ideally, it is here the play's issues are brought into their clearest, sharpest focus. Like the wave breaking on the shore, it will be seen to grow out of all the preceding action. It will often appear to gather together all the striking scenes that have gone before and replay them at speed.

Examples are the storm on the heath in *King Lear*; the banishment of Coriolanus; the trial scenes of *The Merchant of Venice* and Arthur Miller's *The Crucible*; the discovery of Lady Teazle behind the screen in Sheridan's *The School for Scandal*, and of Mrs. Erlynne in Lord Darlington's rooms in Wilde's *Lady Windermere's Fan*; and the open meeting when Dr. Stockmann confronts the townspeople in Ibsen's *An Enemy of the People*.

Climactic Range

It is wrong however to assume that a play's structure automatically has a graph shaped like a pyramid. Many have a major climactic range with a double apex or more: *Julius Caesar*, with the assassination followed by Antony's oration; *Macbeth*, with the murder of

Duncan, then the banquet scene; the banishment of Coriolanus, followed by his march on Rome and the play's final great reversal.

In Arthur Miller's *Death of a Salesman*, the past and present streams of action hit their climax together in the scene in the restaurant the day Willy Loman is fired. As his two sons desert him, his imagination fills with the scene in the Boston hotel room fifteen years before, when his elder son's idolatry was shattered on finding a woman there.

Resolution

The unwinding after the climax—the resolution, the unraveling, or denouement—although less exciting, is extremely absorbing. It too must grow naturally out of the plot. The impact of the major crisis we have just witnessed on the people involved in it must ring true. If it does not, then the situation itself was very likely untrue. The whole process must seem probable, necessary, and inevitable.

The final reaction of an audience to a dramatic action, perfectly rounded out and complete, is not really one of surprise, however stunned they may be. In Arthur Miller's phrase, it is "Oh God, of course!"

A Streetcar Named Desire

At the climax of Tennessee Williams' *A Streetcar Named Desire*, Blanche DuBois is raped by the brutal Stanley Kowalski. It is the culminating point of a series of disasters for her. The author resolves his play with inexorable logic. In the final scene Blanche is led away to a mental institution by a doctor and nurse. Her sister, Stanley's wife, cannot bring herself to believe Blanche's story and has had her committed. But Blanche has, in any event, been forced during the play to confront her own nymphomania. Her fine illusions of the past, her fantasies of gentility, and her dreams of a respectable marriage have been destroyed. Only by crossing the borders of sanity can she reinstate them.

Waste

By the last act of Granville Barker's *Waste*, the career of Henry Trebell, the brilliant independent MP, has been wrecked by scandal.

The passion of his life, a Bill for Church Disestablishment, will never be born—just as his child will never be born because the adulteress, who was carrying it, died after an abortion. Trebell's suicide at the play's end is a shock, but from what we have seen of his uncompromising nature, and from the evidence of his last conversation with his devoted sister, Granville Barker's resolution is totally in character and grows naturally out of everything which has gone before.

The Crucible

The witch hunt in Arthur Miller's *The Crucible* reaches its terrifying climax in the court examination. John Proctor's furious attack on his accusers and defense of his wife rebound on him, and he is thrown into jail. His refusal to save his own life by selling his friends in the last act of the play is dramatically convincing. It renders back his self-esteem and, now reconciled with his wife, it finally frees him from his guilt. He chooses death because there is no other way for a man of conscience and integrity. The play's resolution has an impressive dignity. (The initial driver of the action is of course Abigail Williams, the chief crier of "witch," and Proctor's sometime mistress.)

Scene Structure: Kattrin's Drum

Individual scenes often parallel the action of the whole. A scene will have a rising movement, a climax, and a falling movement. In Brecht's *Mother Courage*, Kattrin, Courage's mute daughter, tries to warn the town of Halle that a night attack by Catholic troops is coming. She climbs on the roof of a peasant's house and starts beating a drum. The soldiers try every way to stop her without violence, but their options close. She is out of reach and has pulled up the ladder. The noise of the drum cannot be drowned in any natural way like chopping wood, and threats to destroy her wagon will not work. The drum beats get more frenetic.... Finally the soldiers have no alternative. A musket is set up on forks, and Kattrin is shot dead. This is the climax of the scene. But she has succeeded. The sound of alarm bells and gunfire rising from the town show it will not be taken by surprise.

The Pound of Flesh

In the trial scene from *The Merchant of Venice* (Act IV, Scene 1) the climax is the moment when Portia tells Shylock he cannot shed one drop of blood in securing his bond. Before this turning point, Antonio's mortal danger increases every second as Portia leads Shylock into a false belief that, according to the laws of Venice, his victory is certain. From this point, Shylock's fortunes plunge downward, and he leaves the court a broken man.

Objectives in Comedy

The action in a comedy is just as important as in all other forms of drama. The plot is as solidly built. But the objectives should not be treated with deep seriousness by the audience. (They are serious enough for the characters of course.) Near the end of Shaw's *You Never Can Tell,* Bohun QC tells Crampton: "Your notion of going to law is all nonsense: your children will be of age before you can get the point decided." In that case, what has the last act been about? It chiefly exists for Shaw to import the magnificent booming Bohun to bounce all the main characters about in a highly entertaining way until he meets his match in Dolly Clandon.

The main characters in *As You Like It* are in the Forest of Arden essentially to "fleet the time carelessly as they did in the golden world." (The official objective is to escape from Duke Frederick.) There is indeed a fiendishly complicated set of objectives in Congreve's *The Way of the World,* which centers on the struggle to get Lady Wishfort's estates. Most members of the audience, however, decline to tax their brains over this and prefer to enjoy the antics and wit of the characters.

Monsieur Jourdain

In *Le Bourgeois Gentilhomme,* Molière strings together a number of scenes illustrating the attempts of a foolish bourgeois M. Jourdain to ape the manners of the aristocracy. (A man striving for a difficult, indeed impossible, objective.) They advance the story very little—they are virtually revue sketches. But these are the scenes which playgoers delight in and remember. The movement of the play is fueled by them. The audience is eager for more and remains in a state of expectancy.

The writer of comedy deals in comic collisions, ludicrous incongruity, hilarious disproportion between man's aspiration and his performance, and painfully funny embarrassments. He guides his characters into these situations often on very slight pretexts. But the basic principles of dramatic action still apply.

What Is a Play?

A single, all-purpose definition of what a play *is* defies composition. But one may be ventured, combining the basic dramatic principles, which may help new writers.

A play is a dynamic process of change, an arc of movement containing many subsidiary movements, in which a forceful driving agent activates opposing forces of equal strength. It may include the inner processes of thought, perception, and emotion by which a deed comes into being, as well as its impact on the external world. In the protracted struggle of the driving force to achieve its objectives, there are decisive alternations of fortune in which action determines character and character determines action, while the audience, its interest and sympathies strongly engaged, is held throughout in a state of expectancy and uncertainty (suspense). The struggle is resolved logically after the climactic peaks of the action, often with the downfall or death of the central character—and the process is over.

DRAMATIC
TENSION
AND SUSPENSE

3

Tension

"A great part of the secret of dramatic architecture," wrote William Archer, "lies in the one word 'Tension.' To engender, maintain, suspend, heighten, and resolve a state of tension is the main object of the dramatist's craft."

What do we mean by tension? It is a condition of mental stress or excitement. The mind is actually stretched. The pulse probably beats faster. It is, of course, an essential element of suspense, which has been called the nerve center or the mainspring of drama. The two are not strictly synonymous, for there are instances of dramatic tension where the suspense factor does not commonly apply.

Suspense

For immediate practical purposes, however, George Pierce Baker's definition of suspense is valuable:

> Suspense means a straining forward of interest, a compelling desire to know what will happen next. When a hearer is totally at a loss to

know what will happen, but is eager to ascertain; when he partly guesses what will take place, but deeply desires to make sure; or he almost holds back so greatly does he dread an anticipated situation, he is in a state of suspense, for, be it willingly or unwillingly on his part, on sweeps his interest.

The Wild Duck

Suspense implies an imminent reversal of fortune. The Sword of Damocles hangs over the head of the protagonist. Or, if you like, a time bomb is ticking. In Ibsen's *The Wild Duck*, Gregers Werle enters Hjalmar Ekdal's home as a lodger. We know he will wreck the happiness of everyone in it. Hjalmar is blissfully unaware that his wife was once the mistress of Gregers' father, Haakon Werle, and that his young daughter Hedvig is not his own. Gregers' perverted idealism is bound to construe it as his duty to tell Hjalmar the truth. But it is a long time before he makes his first move. Ibsen well knows that the audience will be on the edge of their seats by then.

In Ingmar Bergman's production of the play, Max von Sydow, as Gregers, started his long chat with Hedvig at a good distance from her across the stage. As the talk charmingly proceeded, he moved closer and closer to her: a chilling image of danger.

Milking Situations: Dogberry in *Much Ado*

The "milking" of situations involves suspense, particularly in comedy; for example, making a character, previously established as given to verbosity, take a long time to deliver or fail to deliver a vital piece of news—Constable Dogberry in *Much Ado About Nothing* (Act III Scene 5). The clown has already unwittingly stumbled on the plot to wreck Hero's wedding, and he goes with Verges to see Hero's father, Leonato, the governor of the city. But he never gets to the point because he is so swollen with self-importance, verbose, and totally lacking in any sense of priorities. Verges tries to break through his monumental circumlocutions and tell Leonato, but Dogberry shuts him up—he wants to do the talking ("A good old man, sir, he will be talking; as they say, 'when the age is in, the wit is out'"...etc.) Finally Leonato leaves impatiently for the church, where tragedy awaits that could so easily have been prevented.

It is a common fault with beginners to drill away at material that has small dramatic potential. But it is equally wrong to skip over material that could yield far more dramatic mileage. A writer should strive to discover all the possibilities for suspense in a scene, exploit the full temperamental range of his characters, and examine how each might affect all the others.

Sympathy

Suspense requires sympathy with the characters. If we do not care for them, it does not much matter if they do suffer a severe reversal. We will not be kept in alternating states of hope and fear about them.

Asking Questions

Most of all, suspense makes the audience ask questions. The movement of a play is from question to answer, from problem to solution. Will Hamlet kill the King before the King kills him? Will Lady Teazle be discovered behind the screen? If so, what will be her reaction—and that of the others on stage? We sense the imminent doom of Oedipus, but just how, and when, and by whom will this be brought about?

The Man Who Came to Dinner

In the Kaufman and Hart Broadway comedy *The Man Who Came to Dinner*, Sheridan Whiteside, a caustic, larger-than-life literary personality, breaks his hip and is trapped for weeks with a family in the Midwest. Much of the plot is concerned with Whiteside's efforts to prevent his secretary from leaving him to get married. Will playboy Beverly Carlton sabotage Whiteside's plan to stop the marriage? Will the wily Whiteside, who misses nothing, tumble to Carlton's ruse? Amid the flow of hectic talk, Whiteside begins to listen very carefully, putting two and two together; the audience grows increasingly anxious, fearing the gaff will be blown. It is. Again, the suspense depends on our sympathy for the secretary and our wanting Whiteside to lose.

Rope

In Patrick Hamilton's thriller *Rope*, two young psychopaths murder a fellow student just for the thrill of it. They place his body in a chest, then invite his father and other guests to supper—served off the chest, which is in full view throughout. The suspense of course hinges on the question—will the guests discover the body and the murderers be brought to justice? Inevitably the audience's sympathies are with one suspicious man who begins to latch on to the truth.

The Parachute

In David Mercer's television play *The Parachute*, Werner von Reger is preparing for a hazardous jump to test a new parachute. Crucial scenes of his life prior to joining the Luftwaffe are intercut with shots of him assembling his equipment...climbing the parachute tower...reaching the platform. There is a tight framework of suspense for the story based on the questions—Will he jump? If he does, will he be killed?

High Noon

The classic Western *High Noon* combines the tension of waiting with urgent questions. It is less than an hour before the killer's train arrives at noon. Newly pardoned, he is returning to exact revenge on the outgoing marshal who sentenced him to be hanged. His three henchmen wait at the station. There are shots of the empty railway line stretching into the distance, and the hands of the clock moving closer to noon. Meanwhile, the marshal scours the town for deputies. Will he find them? One by one they cry off. If he cannot find them, will he run away? Or will he stay and face almost certain death? Again, we must feel sympathy with the marshal in order to care about the answers. The way he comports himself under stress—and of course the fact that he is played by Gary Cooper—ensures that we do.

Often it is not only What happens next? but What is happening? Why is this happening? What has happened? For example...

After Magritte

Tom Stoppard's comedy *After Magritte* opens with an extraordinary stage tableau. An elderly woman is lying on an ironing board with a black bowler hat on her stomach. A woman in a ball gown kneels on the floor. A large basket of fruit hangs down from the ceiling. A man is standing on a chair, his torso bare, wearing black evening dress trousers and green rubber fishing waders; he is blowing into the lamp shade. A uniformed policeman is gazing at the scene through the window. The audience reaction to this is "What the hell?" That is indeed the question, and the play eventually supplies the answer. At the end the tableau is even more bizarre, but this time we know how it all came about.

Each act of a play except the last (and sometimes that too) ends on a question mark, as does each episode of a radio or television serial. In the television serial *Dallas*—Who shot J.R.?

In *A Chorus Line*—Who will get the jobs?

Dostoevsky

The enormously prolonged suspense of Dostoevsky's *Crime and Punishment* hinges on two questions—Will the police nail Raskolnikov for the murders? Will his terrible guilt force him to confess? We do not know the answer until the very last lines (if we exclude the Epilogue). There are, in fact, only fifteen words after Raskolnikov utters his confession at the police office. It could even be argued that the suspense is held until the last four words: "Raskolnikov repeated his statement."

In tragedy, just how will the inevitable catastrophe be brought about? In romance, will boy get girl? In a detective story, who dunnit? In fact, as long as the audience continues to ask questions, there is a play. As soon as all the questions are answered, the play is over.

Half-Answers

The cunning dramatist—and Hamlet used that adjective in his description of good play writing—will employ half-answers, answers that satisfy less than they intrigue and tantalize, answers that in turn suggest new and still more pressing questions, as when the removal of one obstacle leads to the creation of a larger obstacle. If there is to be growing suspense, new questions—continually suggested by the progressing action—must be created at a faster rate than the answers.

In Shaw's *Pygmalion*, Professor Higgins overcomes all difficulties and successfully introduces Eliza into London society. But this very triumph creates an entirely new crisis in his relationship with the now independent Eliza, which occupies the rest of the play.

Voysey

After Edward Voysey has resolved to grapple with his crushing inheritance, ending the audience's uncertainty on that point, George Booth, an old family friend, comes to him at the end of Act Four and wants to call in all his money. This is because he does not have the same confidence in Edward that he had in his father. It is a new crisis springing directly from Edward's decision to carry on. Edward has no alternative but to tell Booth that his father embezzled most of his money. The new question is: Will the furious George Booth—or any other client who discovers the truth—go to the police? That provides the suspense for Act Five.

The action of a good play is progressive, always unpacking fresh strife and obstacles, new problems growing out of solutions to the old. "Alps on Alps arise."

Mystery and Curiosity

Suspense is therefore closely bound up with mystery. The aim should be to sustain the uncertainties as long as possible. The author does not reveal his hand until it is absolutely necessary. Beckett and Pinter often do not reveal it at all. The creation of pleasing ambiguities, leaving several options open, never being too explicit or giving the game away too early, is a major portion of dramatic technique. It is the art of withholding information.

Withholding Information

The author rations his information, not disclosing anything before it is needed. In a celebrated thriller of the 1920s, *The Man in the Dark* by John Ferguson, the hero is witness to a murder, but with a catch: It is cleverly concealed until deep in the narrative that he is blind.

At the end of a scene in *Twelfth Night* (Act II, Scene 3), Maria gives Sir Toby Belch only a bare outline of her plot against Malvolio. No mention of yellow stockings or crossed garters here. The rich details are saved for the next scene but one, when we witness the whole process by which Malvolio is ensnared.

There is clearly something strange about Aston in Harold Pinter's play *The Caretaker*. But we do not know exactly what it is until his long speech at the end of Act Two. Much curiosity and suspense is gained by delaying the revelation.

When a new act of a play begins, the playwright will be in no hurry to answer the questions posed at the end of the previous act. He thus intensifies the interest and curiosity of the audience. *The Wild Duck* has more than one notable example.

We do not know until the very end of Frederick Forsyth's *The Day of the Jackal* just how the killer intends to assassinate de Gaulle, though this has been his mission from the outset. The tension would have been taken out of the narrative if we had learned it at an earlier stage.

Explain Later

A plane crash is more dramatic than what the black box reveals afterward.

If an event is dramatic in itself, the explanation can wait until later. If it is attached at the same time, it will clog the action, and an opportunity will be missed to keep curiosity alive. Many plays and films begin with a short violent burst of action, the meaning of which the audience is quite content to be told later.

A dead body is hurled off a train; a witty encounter takes place at a skiing resort between a suave stranger and a beautiful young woman; the woman arrives back in Paris to find her house has been stripped bare; she is told by the police her husband is dead, that he had left home in a hurry, and had several different passports with different aliases; at his funeral three strange men arrive independently and make sure he is dead, one by sticking a pin into him. This is how the film *Charade* opens. Neither we nor the young woman know what it is all about, but we are intrigued, disturbed, and amused. We stay with the film to know more.

Dramatic Ambiguity

Dramatic ambiguity in plotting casts its own unique spell. In Harold Pinter's play *The Collection*, did Stella sleep with Bill in Leeds? They may have, or they may have just talked about it. Their partners are desperate to know the answer, but the play never gives it. It is left open. In the same author's *Old Times*, Deeley and his wife's best friend, Anna, compete to possess his wife through cherished memories of their early lives together. But did those events really happen? As they try to cap, and even steal each other's memories, and as many years have elapsed, the past becomes open to very different interpretations. The uncertainty heightens the tension.

An author's ambivalence toward his characters can have formidable dramatic results, as can his ambivalence toward his own professed philosphy. Brecht imposed an iron Marxist discipline on his violent anarchic spirit. This tension created a subtle ambiguity in his plays that leaves them open to different readings. Certainly, state communism has never felt at ease with the plays. But their power in the theater is undeniable.

Suspense and Surprise

The superiority of suspense to surprise is worth emphasizing. The playwright has a better ally in the complicity of the audience than in its ignorance. Using the bomb example again, the time it is really effective is before it explodes, not after.

If we know a bomb is planted under a conference table, we watch the entire proceedings in a high state of tension, and still get a shock when it goes off. If we do not know it is there, a minute's worth of shock is obtained when it explodes, compared with many minutes worth of suspense in the other instance. Hitchcock, the cinematic master of suspense, rarely bothers to explode his bomb at all. His theory in this respect is considered in a later section.

Retardation

For all the unease and edginess created by suspense, it is pleasurable. Percival Wilde wrote in *The Craftsmanship of the One-Act Play*:

> Drama is motion. Suspense is the tantalizing pleasure produced by artistically retarding that motion. How much to retard, and when, finally, to fling off restraint, and plunge into satisfying action—these are questions which the dramatist can answer only by transcending the barriers of self, and resolving to see his work precisely as an audience will see it.

This tantalizing pleasure survives several visits to a fine play or film. We know the outcome, but we still enjoy the tension at a third or fourth viewing.

Relaxation of Tension

Tension cannot be endured without breaks. As with the pace of a play, variety is needed. Just as a short, fast scene and a long, slow scene both gain by contrast and juxtaposition, so dramatic tension is enhanced by its suspension. The cause of the tension never goes right away; it is always there in the background waiting to return. The tension graph is full of highs and lows, but as a whole it steadily rises. There is danger perhaps. It comes close, then veers away; relief follows, but the audience feels uneasy. When will it return? The next time it comes in closer, is even more scary, then it swings away again. The film *Jaws*, in which a killer shark terrorizes an East Coast resort, is a good example. Or a ghost story. We know the ghost will appear again. But when?

The Wages of Fear

In Clouzot's original film *The Wages of Fear* (1953), four men, badly in need of money, are given the highly dangerous mission of driving two truck loads of nitro-glycerine explosive across the rough roads of South America. It is needed to put out a fire at an oilfield several hundred miles away. A jolt could set off the explosives at any second of the hazardous journey. (Objective: to get there alive and put out the fire.) After a prolonged hair-raising episode, in which the four use some of the nitro-glycerine to blow up a large rock that blocks the road (literally a formidable obstacle), there is a short interlude of wild relief and hilarity. The men line up and urinate into a ditch (relaxation of tension). The audience laughs uproariously. The two lorries, spaced well apart, continue smoothly on their journey. It is precisely at this point that the leading lorry explodes, and its two occupants are killed instantly.

Scène à Faire

Expectations about characters, once aroused, should normally be satisfied; otherwise the audience can feel cheated. If it has been led to expect, for example, a major confrontation, then that scene becomes virtually obligatory. This has been termed the *scène à faire*. If everything has pointed toward it and it is then never shown, disappointment and a sense of let-down usually result that are fatal to the success of the play. The author has not delivered what he promised.

The Wild Duck

This however is not an invariable requirement. In *The Wild Duck*, Ibsen staged his *scène à faire* offstage, when Gregers reveals the truth about Hjalmar's marriage to him. He simply takes him out for a long walk at the end of Act Three. We never witness the disclosure. When the curtain rises on Act Four, nothing immediately appears to have changed. We are aware however that Hjalmar has received a shock. By crafting the play thus, Ibsen has doubled the suspense. Just how much did Gregers tell Hjalmar? We sense a tragedy is still to come, but we do not know what it is or how it will be brought about. Ibsen makes us wait.

Unsatisfied Expectation

There are cases where expectation is never satisfied. Enclosed within Kafka's story *The Great Wall of China* there is a fable in which a messenger from the dying Emperor is sent out through the multitudes cramming the mazes and labyrinths of the palace. But because the chambers and corridors and courtyards of the palace are endless, the message can never reach the city, let alone the outlying provinces. Yet we are all the time willing it to happen. This opposition—the urgent drive of the messenger, and the impossibility of his ever achieving his objective—generates a powerful tension. So does K's endless quest in *The Castle*, met by endless frustration.

The simple fact of waiting creates tension. In *Waiting for Godot*, Beckett sustains the tension throughout the whole play, because of course Godot never comes.

This expectation, this willing for something to break, on the part of the spectator or the reader, and its resolute denial by the author is the equivalent of the strongly willed purpose and the formidable obstacle mentioned above. Nothing may "happen" in the conventional sense, no goal be reached; but high tensions are established, and also internal conflict in the minds of the audience. And this is dramatic.

Attendant Lords

Tom Stoppard's *Rosencrantz and Guildenstern are Dead*, which was influenced by *Waiting for Godot*, works on the same principles. The two "attendant lords" of the title spend most of their time waiting in ante-rooms at the beck and call of great personages. They have to pass the time somehow. They play word games. They philosophize. They talk about Hamlet. They bicker. The first few minutes of the play consist of the pair betting on the toss of a coin. They even talk about the art of building up suspense in relation to this. When Rosencrantz and Guildenstern are used by the Great Ones, they are no wiser as to their real purpose at the Court, or indeed in life. But the audience still *expects*. It remains held in a state of tension. Eventually, of course, something does happen to the pair: they are killed. But they never know why.

Fierce expectation—our willing hard for something to break, and its iron denial by the dramatist—is, of course, what creates the extraordinary tension throughout *Hamlet* itself.

Tension and Suspense

If a fine distinction were to be drawn, tension can exist without the suspense factor. Tension is an internal dynamic that need not be related to an outside event. It can exist without a threat hanging overhead. Nor is it necessary to expect anything to happen at the end of a tense passage of dialogue. It is all happening within the dialogue.

A man and his wife are having a tense conversation. The cause of the tension is never stated. It may be another woman—we don't know. We are not led to expect a violent conclusion to the scene. But tension is still generated.

Erotic tension, the tension of a nightmare, the tension of hostility can all exist without the Sword of Damocles or a sense of time running out.

Metamorphosis

In Kafka's nightmarish *Metamorphosis*, Gregor Samsa, transmuted into a giant insect, desperately wants to get out of bed and answer his family knocking on the door. But he cannot. The opposition of his straining to rise with the refusal of his new body to obey create a vise-like tension. But it is not a conventional suspense situation.

The suspense is there, of course, if we look for it. It is both distant and very close. The ultimate question is: What will be the reaction of his family when they see him? The immediate question is: Will Samsa be able to hoist himself without arms? Intermediate questions include his own fears about being late for work and losing his job. The suspense framework is like a number of concentric circles.

Wheels within Wheels

This applies in general to the fortunes of supporting characters as well as the protagonist. There are smaller and smaller dramas going on inside the main action, wheels within wheels.

The definition of suspense can in fact be extended to include minutely graded steps. An audience will follow with intense interest the least alteration in an erotic power struggle; for example, will Lenny in Harold Pinter's *The Homecoming* get Ruth to surrender her glass of water to him?

Suspense Line by Line

The line-by-line suspense of a passage of dialogue might have an audience thinking "Now, what will he say to that?" or "Did that remark wound her?" or "Who will win this rally?" It can be a conversational minefield. In this passage from the first scene of Edward Albee's *Who's Afraid of Virginia Woolf?*, suspense occurs line by line over just when and how George will get savaged by Martha for being insufficiently enthusiastic about the joke at the party:

Who's Afraid of Virginia Woolf?

GEORGE: It was all right, Martha....

MARTHA: You laughed your head off when you heard it at the party.

GEORGE: I smiled. I didn't laugh my head off...I smiled, you know? ...it was all right.

MARTHA: (*gazing into her drink*): You laughed your goddamn head off.

GEORGE: It was all right...

MARTHA: (*ugly*): It was a scream!

GEORGE: (*patiently*): It was very funny; yes.

MARTHA: (*after a moment's consideration*): You make me puke!

GEORGE: What?

MARTHA: Uh...you make me puke!

GEORGE: (*thinks about it...then...*): That wasn't a very nice thing to say, Martha.

MARTHA: That wasn't *what*?

GEORGE: ...a very nice thing to say.

MARTHA: I like your anger. I think that's what I like about you most... your anger. You're such a...such a simp! You don't even have the...the what?...

GEORGE: ...guts?...

MARTHA: PHRASEMAKER! (*Pause...then they both laugh*)

Word by Word

Suspense can be concentrated word by word. A detective tries to catch a dying man's last words, so that he can name his murderer. A great statesman, now senile, struggles to get through a speech in the House of Commons: each word, each pause adds to the pain and tension of the situation.

The better the writer, the more suspense, because he can strike the audience with a surprising choice of word. A character speaking slowly and thoughtfully, but with immense verbal precision, is very suspenseful. Albee is a master here.

But a character does not need to be articulate to have an audience hanging on every word. In Harold Pinter's *The Caretaker*, Aston, in his long speech at the end of the second act, describes how he was forcibly given electric shock treatment in a hospital. He cannot phrase the effect on his mind. But his efforts to do so hold the theater in total silence.

> The trouble was...my thoughts...had become very slow...I couldn't think at all...I couldn't...get...my thoughts...together ...uuuhh...I could...never quite get it...together.

Suspense can even be achieved letter by letter. A character stammers. What is the word he is trying to say? If it is not in the text, the actor can sometimes impose a stammer, as Olivier did in his performance as Hotspur in *Henry IV*, and at a crucial moment in *Othello* (see page 147).

EXPOSITION

4

Inspector Hound

In Tom Stoppard's comedy, *The Real Inspector Hound*, with its splendid take-off on the stage detective thriller, the charwoman, Mrs. Drudge, answers the phone at the beginning with the words: "Hello, the drawing room of Lady Muldoon's country residence one morning in early spring."

She notices Simon Gascoyne at the window, starts talking to him, and the following exchange takes place:

MRS. DRUDGE: ...Judging by the time, (*she glances at the clock*) you did well to get here before high water cut us off for all practical purposes from the outside world.

SIMON: I took the short cut over the cliffs and followed one of the old smugglers' paths through the treacherous swamps that surround this strangely inaccessible house.

MRS. DRUDGE: Yes, many visitors have remarked on the topographical quirk in the local strata whereby there are no roads leading from the Manor, though there ARE ways of getting TO it, weather allowing.

Why is this funny? Because it burlesques appallingly mishandled dramatic technique. A playwright has a certain amount of factual information about present circumstances and past events that he must convey to the audience, if they are to understand and enter into the spirit of the action that follows. He could take the easy way out and provide a long program note or a prologue, but most audiences rightly dislike this arid procedure. They prefer to have the information built into the story.

Ideally, the audience should absorb knowledge without realizing they are doing so. If chunks of information are stuffed arbitrarily into the dialogue, the effect on natural speech and characterization will be disastrous. Ultimately it becomes nonsense. In the previous excerpt there is no reason whatever why Mrs. Drudge and Simon should tell each other all these things.

The classic example of bad exposition is when two supernumeraries are discovered at curtain rise, and one proceeds to retail a stream of facts which the other would be bound to know already.

Deep Background

It may not, of course, be necessary to have a formal exposition. The facts will become clear in the natural course of the play, or they will be inferred from what is seen and heard. In exceptional instances the whole background story need never be spelled out at all if the dramatist is skillful enough. The audience is so enthralled by the conflicts and tensions engendered that the past history of the characters can remain shadowy. But it is still important. The background story of a play by Harold Pinter may not be explicit but it can reveal much on close examination, and go far toward explaining the "menace" which is axiomatic when talking about his work.

Exposition by Contention

Successful exposition is often presented in the form of conflict. It may, for example, emerge as a furious denial of something that is asserted or a defense of someone who is attacked.

Molière's *The Misanthrope* plunges into the middle of the action, which is also acutely expository. The uncompromising Alceste is arguing fiercely with his friend Philinte, accusing him of hypocrisy for warmly embracing a man he despises. The argument ranges over several topics, including Alceste's love for the fickle Célimène. Why does he love her, asks Philinte, if he demands total honesty in human relations? In a few concentrated minutes, Molière declares the essential conflict of character and manners that will dominate the play to come.

Expository Devices

Inventive expository devices are an important part of play construction. An expository device, to be truly successful, must be invisible. It must seem perfectly natural that the facts should come out in the way they do. The device must be interesting in itself, quite apart from the information the spectator gathers from it. He is again not conscious that background facts are being insinuated into his mind.

The dialogue of a good expository device is colored with emotion and is marked by characterizing incident.

Sweet Bird of Youth

In the first scene of *Sweet Bird of Youth* by Tennessee Williams, a gigolo, Chance Wayne, tries to blackmail the Princess, an aging former movie star, by secretly tape recording her incriminating admissions about the use of hashish, which she has smuggled into the country. In the course of this (striving to attain a difficult objective) he also draws out of her the central facts of her life and personality, including her relationship with him, which an audience needs for an understanding of the drama. The exposition of these facts is Tennessee Williams' main purpose. The blackmail is the expository device by which he achieves it.

Dear Brutus

The playwright's most effective recourse is to make the audience *demand* the exposition. He arranges it that the audience is eager to know what he wishes to exposit.

In the first act of *Dear Brutus*, Barrie wishes to convey to the audience that a strange little man, Lob, has gathered a group of strangers together at his house in Midsummer week for a mysterious purpose.

Barrie starts off with nothing to do with this. The ladies of the company are talking about the loss of some jewelry. They know their rings have been stolen, and they know the butler, Matey, is the culprit. After some discussion, in which the bolder spirits prevail over the more timid, they decide to confront the butler. Threatened with the police, he admits the theft and returns the rings. The ladies then say they will still inform the police unless he tells them why Lob has invited them to the house and what it is they all have in common. Even so, he clams up and will give only a few dark hints and warnings. By now the audience is extremely curious, and the play is under way.

Hedda Gabler

In the first act of *Hedda Gabler*, there is much background information Ibsen wishes to convey about Eilert Loevborg. He does it by making Hedda—who, it is hinted, has had some emotional involvement with Loevborg in the past, though we do not know to what degree—worm the facts out of Mrs. Elvsted.

Mrs. Elvsted is evasive about the real reason for her appearance in town. Hedda gradually forces the truth from her by subtle, persistent interrogation (a will pitted against an obstacle). We are soon just as keen as Hedda to know more about Loevborg. What is Mrs. Elvsted hiding? What was Hedda's relationship with Loevborg in the past? And Mrs. Elvsted's with him now? The audience is eagerly asking the questions, the answers to which constitute the play's exposition.

More than this, the exposition is action. It becomes clear that Loevborg's arrival could be explosive. We have seen that Hedda is already bored with her marriage to Tesman. If she and Loevborg meet, it could prove fatal to Mrs. Elvsted's happiness. Loevborg, cured of drink, is also a potential threat to Tesman's career. And Loevborg's new way of life and happiness are themselves in danger, because our suspicions are confirmed, at the end of the act, that the woman in his past who tried to shoot him was Hedda herself.

So, as the exposition proceeds, there is change taking place before our eyes. There is growing conflict, the unveiling of character under emotional stress, and a sense of bad trouble looming. In a word, action.

Exposition Equals Action

Both Ibsen and Sophocles characteristically begin their plays about four-fifths of the way through the story, a short time before the crisis. The unveiling of the past becomes not a mere recital of information but a series of revelations which gun the action forward with an increasing sense of danger. We are offered, as Arthur Miller puts it, "the marvelous spectacle of life forcing one event out of the jaws of the preceding one."

Oedipus Rex is the supreme example, where the exposition is held back as long as possible and released at the moment of maximum dramatic impact. The height of the drama is when the King forces the truth out of the old shepherd about the events surrounding his own birth, at the very beginning of the story. And this precipitates the catastrophe.

The Crucible

A final example from Arthur Miller shows how, in a superb play, action and exposition are indistinguishable. The curtain rises on the first act of *The Crucible* when the action has already begun and is gathering momentum. Witches are suspected in Salem. Fear walks the town. A group of local girls have participated in an obscene diabolic ritual in the woods at night. One of the girls, the daughter of Reverend Parris, has fallen into a mysterious coma. Is she bewitched? The whole act takes place in her bedroom, and she becomes a magnet for most of the important personages in the play. Quarrels flare up among them, fed by envy, greed, lust, and hatred. These collisions tell us much about their characters, important events in their past, and the social and religious climate of the time; and they prepare for the terror and hysteria to come. It is almost churlish to call Betty Parris' bed, which is the focal point of the action, an expository device. The audience is so caught up in what is happening, no one stops to consider it. And that is as it should be.

PREPARATION

5

"The art of the theater is the art of preparations" said the younger Dumas. Preparing an audience skillfully so that it will immediately grasp, appreciate, and be moved by decisive events later in the play is a vital ingredient of play making. An audience cannot be made to feel strongly about things that have not been made clear to them, and a crisis is wasted on them unless they are prepared for it.

Atmosphere

Atmosphere and tone are part of preparation, ominousness particularly—the casting of a long warning shadow. In only twelve lines, the first scene of *Macbeth* vividly creates the whole spirit of the tragedy to come.

At the start of *Death of a Salesman*, the sad tune played on a flute in the distance "telling of grass and trees and the horizon," and the image of the little man trudging back home at night, bowed down with his cases of samples, sets the tone of the play superbly.

The same can be said of Chekhov's use of nature to convey lost happiness. The lake in *The Seagull* is such a strong presence that the author is supposed to have regarded it as one of the characters. In *The Cherry Orchard*, the orchard itself has an even more compelling influence. It powerfully evokes childhood memories for the family and, at the same time, stands as a symbol for an obsolete social order soon to be cut down.

Foreshadowing

In a larger sense a playwright can "foreshadow" an event, or a play's tragic end. When Caesar's ghost appears to Brutus (Act IV, Scene 3) and says he will see him at Philippi, the message for Brutus and the audience is clear. The millrace, where Rosmer's first wife committed suicide, is well emphasized in Ibsen's *Rosmersholm*, foreshadowing the joint tragedy at the play's end when Rebecca and Rosmer throw themselves into it. Chekhov said if you produce a revolver in Act One, you imply that someone will be shot in Act Three.

Preparation has other names: "sign-posting"; "planting" a fact needed in the plot later; "establishing" a point or mood; "setting up" a situation.

Falstaff

In the first part of *Henry IV*, the charade that Falstaff and Prince Hal enact in the Boar's Head (Act II, Scene 4)—in which the Prince, playing his father, orders the banishment of Falstaff—prepares for the eventual banishment of Falstaff in reality by Prince Hal when he becomes King. A cruder form of preparation is employed earlier in Hal's soliloquy "Yet herein will I imitate the sun," at the end of the play's second scene, when he says he will eventually ditch all his tavern companions. It is so crude it alienates the audience from Prince Hal and damages the play. Unlike the charade, it is a bad piece of craftsmanship.

Motivation

Preparation is very evident in well-motivated characterization. If a man is established early in the play by one or two minor incidents as having a violent nature when roused, it will be immediately plausible at the play's climax if he murders someone in a fit of rage. Preparation establishes motivation and makes the play believable.

Suspending Disbelief

Preparation suspends disbelief. If it is well planted—as in the Western *True Grit*—that the hero is legendary for winning against desperate odds, then the audience will happily accept an absurd feat of derring-do at a crucial point later.

Othello

The main reason why we accept Othello's manipulation by Iago, and do not dismiss his gullibility out of hand as being implausible, is that nearly half the play is devoted to showing how successfully Iago does manipulate people in general. Roderigo, Brabantio, Cassio, Montano, Emilia, Desdemona—all do what he makes them want to do. When the action begins in earnest, with the line, "Ha! I like not that." no one questions Iago's power over individuals, Othello included.

Here, as usual, he gets others to do most of his work for him. Desdemona herself lays the groundwork for the temptation scene when she vehemently urges Othello to forgive the disgraced Cassio. She does this because Cassio has begged her to do so, an idea suggested to him by Iago. In the temptation scene itself, Othello virtually has to drag the lie out of Iago. For a long time he gives only veiled hints that he knows more than he is willing to speak.

The Double Value

Successful preparation, it was argued by Percival Wilde, employs incidents and plot points that have a double value. The real value lies hidden in the mind of the dramatist until he is ready to spring it on the audience later in the play. The ostensible value, sufficient always to justify its existence, makes it entertaining and interesting in itself when first presented.

In *The Barretts of Wimpole Street* by Rudolph Besier, for example, it is established early on that Elizabeth is extremely fond of her dog, Flush. This is interesting in itself because it shows the heroine's warmth and kindness and involves some diverting "business." This is the ostensible value which would alone justify its inclusion in the play. But its real value comes at the famous final curtain. After learning that Elizabeth has eloped with Robert Browning, her tyrannical father suddenly sees how to get his revenge—he will destroy her dog. Elizabeth's sister with undisguised triumph then announces that Elizabeth's letter to her says they have taken Flush with them. It is always guaranteed to raise a cheer from the audience.

The ostensible value of the preparatory point should be thought about just as much as its real value. In *The Man Who Came to Dinner*, Whiteside regularly receives bizarre presents from admirers—at one point four live penguins are delivered to the house. Each present creates a funny incident which can be enjoyed for its own sake. The real value emerges in the last act when an Egyptian mummy case is delivered and offers the ideal way to spirit Lorraine—the main obstacle to a happy ending—out of town.

The ostensible value of the point avoids giving the game away. When it has an immediate relevance, the audience is unlikely to look too hard for its ultimate purpose.

Dangers

Shrewd judgment is always needed in preparation. It can go seriously wrong. It can be grossly overdone, for example. Max Beerbohm, reviewing Jerome K. Jerome's *The Passing of the Third Floor Back*, said that he knew what was going to happen, how it was going to happen, and then, as soon as it had happened, that it would happen again.

Too obvious preparation is self-defeating. Once again, the internal mechanics of the plot are showing. Archer wrote: "The clumsiest thing a dramatist can possibly do is to lay a long and elaborate train for the ignition of a squib."

Up the Garden Path

The general superiority of suspense to surprise has already been stressed. But surprise can be very effective in drama if it is cleverly done. Preparation is important here in setting up the audience: red herrings; leading people, through accepted conventions of narrative, in a false direction; making them believe a play is about one thing, until it is suddenly revealed to be about something else altogether.

Pirandello and Genet

Pirandello and Genet are masters of this particular technique; and it is one of the most favored devices in detective stories and thrillers.

For most of his play *Henry IV*, Pirandello makes the audience believe that his hero is mad—he has been incarcerated in a villa for twenty years, thinking he is the Emperor Henry IV of Germany. The dramatist then stuns them with the truth of his returned sanity. Almost before the audience or his visitors have time to recover, the "Emperor" murders his rival in love, and is thus condemned to act out his insane role for the rest of his life.

In his play *The Maids*, Genet begins with a long sequence in which an aristocratic lady torments her maid; then he suddenly reveals that both women are in fact maids (and sisters) who have been play-acting while their mistress is absent from the house.

Psycho

A writer or director can even lead an audience to expect one kind of story and then hit them with a totally different kind of story. For the first half-hour of *Psycho*, Hitchcock prepares us for a conventional cops-and-robbers tale. The very idea that this vital, beautiful girl will not survive the film is unthinkable. Then suddenly, shockingly, she is murdered in the shower, and the film swings into a new dimension.

The advantage of a televison play over a film or a play in the theater is that millions experience the surprise at the same moment. Critics and word-of-mouth have had no opportunity to reveal it.

Thrillers and Detectives

Detective stories and thrillers are, in fact, excellent examples of dramatic structure. Here, in colorful profusion, are to be found quests for truth, the planting of clues, tough obstacles, blind alleys, suspense, mystery, red herrings, twists, reversals, and discoveries. It is no accident that Brecht was very fond of reading Edgar Wallace.

Ionesco, always fascinated by the nature of drama and ready to define it in his plays, says, in *Victims of Duty*:

> All the plays that have ever been written, from Ancient Greece to the present day, have never really been anything but thrillers. Drama's always been realistic and there's always been a detective about. Every play's an investigation brought to a successful conclusion. There's a riddle, and it's solved in the final scene. Sometimes earlier. You seek, and then you find.

The classics, adds Ionesco, are simply "refined detective drama."

Indeed, who can deny that *Oedipus Rex* is a detective story par excellence; that *Hamlet* is an exciting ghost story, full of thrills and suspense?

John le Carré's famous spy thriller *The Spy Who Came in from the Cold* is a treasury of dramatic technique. After reading it through, it is rewarding to analyze its plot structure backwards.

It has an ingenious formula that involves a brilliant reversal: A and B plot to kill C, but in reality it is a plot by A and C to kill B. It is the mainspring of Ira Levin's *Deathtrap*, Clouzot's film *The Fiends*, and indirectly Frederick Knott's *Dial M for Murder*.

EMPHASIS AND CONTRAST

6

Preparation is linked with emphasis. Repetition, elaborate treatment, or the placement given to an event or plot point, will underline it, so that it stays in the memory.

Repetition

Repetition may seem a crude device, but when an audience has to catch words on the wing, it is necessary to ensure that important points, relationships between characters, and significant motivations are very clear in their minds. Great orators believe in saying a thing three times; indeed they often have one point only, which they hammer home again and again.

So it is not overdone for the King's first speech to Hamlet to use the word "father" no less than seven times. It is quite usual for a character to mishear an important word the dramatist wishes to emphasize, or be startled, or fail to comprehend immediately, so that it has to be repeated, for example, when Hedda tells Tesman she still has one thing left to amuse herself with...

HEDDA:	My pistols, George darling.
TESMAN:	Pistols!
HEDDA:	General Gabler's pistols.

Or, in *Othello*:

EMILIA:	...What will you give me now For that same handkerchief?
IAGO:	What handkerchief?
EMILIA:	What handkerchief?

We also see the handkerchief. Emilia makes play with it, bringing it closely to our attention.

Placing

The example from *Hedda Gabler* comes at the very end of the first act, a good point for emphasis. At the start of the second act—another emphatic placing—we see Hedda loading and firing one of the two pistols that will eventually claim both Loevborg's life and, at the very end of the play, her own.

The placing of Mick's sudden reappearance at the end of the first act of *The Caretaker* emphasizes his importance as a character in the play.

Identification

Emphasis is important in identifying characters. At the start of Shaw's *Arms and the Man*, a young woman is standing on a balcony. An older woman enters and calls out "Raina!" twice. The girl turns. Why did the older woman call out her name? Because she wants to attract her attention, yes, but also, very important, because Shaw wishes early to identify the young woman. A few lines later Raina calls the older woman "Mother," so we now know the relationship between them. Unless this is made clear from the start, confusion can result. The dramatist may know who his characters are and their relationship to each other, but the audience will not.

Right emphasis is essential for clarity. Clarity is vital if the audience is to react to the play at all and be moved by it.

There are obvious provisos and exceptions. Emphasis can naturally be overdone, like exposition and preparation, with ludicrous results. Relationships and identities need not be established early, if this arouses curiosity and keeps the audience in a pleasing state of uncertainty.

Edward Bond satirizes the convention of repetition in his play *Restoration*:

LORD ARE: Mrs. Hedges, her ladyship is dead.

MOTHER: Beg pardin sir?

LORD ARE: Her ladyship is dead.

MOTHER: Dead?

LORD ARE: *(aside)*: O the tedium of a tragedy: everything is said twice and then thrice.

MOTHER: Dead?

LORD ARE: *(aside)*: Twice.

MOTHER: Dead!

BOB: Dead!

LORD ARE: *(aside)*: I have survived the morning tolerably well, now I shall spoil it with a headache.

MOTHER: Her ladyship is dead.

LORD ARE: *(aside)*: If she is not she is a consummate actress.

MOTHER: Is her ladyship dead?

LORD ARE: *(aside)*: O god is it to be put to the question? We shall have pamphlets issued on it.

Contrast

An important means of emphasis is contrast—in character and situation.

The hero's sterling qualities in melodrama are emphasized by contrast with the dastardly villain.

As You Like It

Rosalind's impulsive romantic passion in *As You Like It* is highlighted by contrast with the practical, down-to-earth Celia:

CELIA: I found him under a tree, like a dropped acorn.

ROSALIND: It may well be called Jove's tree, when it drops forth such fruit.

CELIA: Give me audience, good madam.

ROSALIND: Proceed.

CELIA: There lay he, stretched along like a wounded knight.

ROSALIND: Though it be pity to see such a sight, it well becomes the ground.

CELIA: Cry 'holla' to thy tongue, I prithee; it curvets unseasonably. He was furnished like a hunter.

ROSALIND: O, ominous! He comes to kill my heart.

CELIA: I would sing my song without a burden; thou bringest me out of tune.

ROSALIND: Do you not know I am a woman? When I think, I must speak.

(Act III, Scene 2)

Antigone

The fierce integrity of Antigone in Sophocles' play is emphasized by contrast with her weak sister Ismene. Ismene is afraid to join Antigone in giving their slain brother an honorable burial, because it offends against the royal edict.

ISMENE: I do not defy them; but I cannot act
Against the State. I am not strong enough.

ANTIGONE: Let that be your excuse, then. I will go
And heap a mound of earth over my brother.

ISMENE: I fear for you, Antigone; I fear—

ANTIGONE: You need not fear for me. Fear for yourself.

ISMENE: At least be secret. Do not breathe a word.
I'll not betray your secret.

ANTIGONE: Publish it
To all the world! Else I shall hate you more.

ISMENE: Your heart burns! Mine is frozen at the thought.

ANTIGONE: I know my duty, where true duty lies.

ISMENE: If you can do it; but you're bound to fail.

ANTIGONE: When I have *tried* and failed, I shall have failed.

Situation Contrast

Contrast of situation is used, for example, in farce when eccentric behavior occurs in an ordinary setting, or normal conduct in bizarre surroundings (Monty Python). It creates dramatic irony in tragedy (Duncan's entry into Macbeth's castle).

Comic irony occurs when the view the playwright takes of his characters contradicts the view they take of themselves. He smiles at them when they are taking themselves most seriously. Self-delusion is the essence of comic characterization—the contrast between what a character is and his image of himself.

Scene Contrast

Scene contrast is vital if the audience's interest is to be kept alive. A long scene followed by a short; a scene of violent action followed by one of calm reflection; a scene in a serious mood followed by one in a lighter vein; a scene that raises hope followed by one that instills fear; a scene of high emotional intensity followed by one that eases the pressure.

Juno and the Paycock

The scene sequence of O'Casey's *Juno and the Paycock* can by turns make an audience laugh (Captain Boyle and Joxer), cry (Mrs. Tancred, Juno), or shiver with fear (the death summons for Johnny). Each is heightened by the contrast.

The Rear Column

Simon Gray's play *The Rear Column*, which charts the slow disintegration of a small group of British officers and gentlemen, cut off in the Congo in 1887, has a quiet, moving moment at the end of the second act, when they all put aside their hatreds and murderous phobias on Christmas Day in an atmosphere of song and good fellowship. We know it will not last, and it makes the final slide into barbarism and madness all the more effective by contrast.

There are, of course, the celebrated Shakespearean comic scenes and characters—the drunken porter in *Macbeth*, the gravediggers in *Hamlet*, and the clown with the figs in *Antony and Cleopatra*—juxtaposed with horror and tragedy.

COMPLICATION

7

Too many first plays fail through lack of complication. They proceed into a too direct line to the outcome. Complications enrich a play, throw it into relief, make it more vivid, prevent it from being palely one dimensional in content. The familiar criticism of a play that it is "too thin" stems from the lack of complications.

A complication in drama generally consists of a new circumstance or character that substantially alters the balance of contending forces—a new weight in the scale. The arrival of Rosencrantz and Guildenstern at Elsinore complicates the plot and swings events in the King's favor. The arrival of the Players complicates the plot still more, swinging things back in Hamlet's favor. The death of Polonius, Hamlet's escape at sea, Laertes' return, and Ophelia's drowning are all complications bearing on the unresolved central issue of the play.

Examples

A complication may create a new love intrigue that cuts across one already going (Puck's intervention in *A Midsummer Night's Dream*).

A love affair complicated by a pregnancy is a perennial dramatic situation.

The complication may come from off the main line of the action. Whatever the fortunes of a group of Russian families prior to 1812, all will be changed by Napoleon's invasion. The lives of a group of American servicemen in Hawaii in 1941 will be totally changed by the Japanese attack on Pearl Harbor.

Mick's arrival at the end of the first act of *The Caretaker* is a complication. Taking the play as a whole, the tramp Davies is a complication in the lives of the two brothers.

A conflict hitherto confined to a close domestic circle may, by the outside world breaking in, come to have social significance and raise high moral issues, as in Terence Rattigan's *The Winslow Boy*, where the supposed theft of a five-shilling postal order by a naval cadet ultimately shakes the government of the day. Or, historically, the constitutional crisis of 1936, leading to the abdication of King Edward VIII.

Something long dormant in a man's character may suddenly spring into action (Macbeth).

A complication suggests additional questions, often of a different nature. New solutions may be possible; or it may now be a bad thing for any solution on the old lines to be found: the feeling that "Things aren't so simple, are they?"

In Maugham's *Home and Beauty*, after the initial complication of the return of the first husband, wrongly presumed killed in the war, it emerges that *neither* husband wants to be married to the heroine.

However, the usual audience reaction to the entry of the complication is "Now what?"

Detaction

Some of the most effective complications lie in ambush for a potential dramatic situation, then detonate it. Percival Wilde wrote:

> Life is full of dramatic situations, but they may exist, without advance, for years. The entrance of a complication is likely to project them so forcibly that vigorous and emphatic movement results. Sometimes the complication is a last straw; sometimes it is an opportunity long and eagerly awaited; sometimes, coming like a thunder-

clap, it is a development bearing so directly upon the situation that sudden and decisive action follows. History, biography, and the daily papers overflow with such examples.

They do indeed: the meeting of the States General in France in May 1789; Sarajevo in 1914; the decision to send Lenin through Germany in a sealed train in 1917; the Nazi–Soviet Pact in August 1939; the Ulster Civil Rights marches in 1968. . . .

In drama, one thinks of the plague and famine gripping Thebes in *Oedipus Rex*; or, in *King Lear*, the placing of Kent in the stocks; or Duncan's sudden decision to stay the night at Macbeth's castle, immediately after confirming the witches' words by making him Thane of Cawdor. Without this last extraordinary combination of circumstances and timing (totally convincing though) Macbeth's ambition and murderousness would have slept on undisturbed. If one factor had been missing—if Macbeth and Banquo had not been out of contact with the rest of the army, if Cawdor had not turned traitor, if Macbeth had met the witches after Ross delivered the news of his elevation—the witches' impact on him, and Lady Macbeth's influence, would have been less, and he would not have killed the King.

SUBJECT, THEME, AND MESSAGE

8

Situations

Where does a writer get ideas for plays? There is a book called *The 36 Dramatic Situations* by Georges Polti which argues, in fact, that there are only thirty-six (headings include Ambition, Revenge, Rivalry in Love, Madness). Goethe and Schiller asserted much the same thing—indeed, they put the number lower. Essentially they are right. The main recurring subjects of drama total about a dozen.

Even if a writer starts with the children of his imagination—his characters—and no plot, he will eventually have to guide them into one. And he will find his choice restricted.

It is impossible to think of a new dramatic situation. The aim should be to get an original angle on it, a fresh variation, a contemporary version. *The Maltese Falcon* and *The French Connection*, for example, are both old-fashioned treasure hunts. Modern cops and robbers are chasing treasure worth millions of dollars—in the first case a sixteenth century golden falcon encrusted with precious gems, in the second a consignment of heroin. It is significant that the Maltese falcon is never found; it remains a chimera, a golden phantasm to lure men to their graves. But what men will do to get it makes for a splendid story.

Any Hollywood film where the small-town girl meets a millionaire in the big city is a Cinderella story (as indeed is *Pygmalion*).

Peter Nichols, the author of *The National Health*, a bitter comedy set in a hospital ward, where patients die from time to time, was influenced by the suspense formula of Agatha Christie's *Ten Little Indians*, where the characters are murdered one by one. Who will go next?

Grand Themes

The word "ideas," though convenient, is not exact. It implies grand themes and concepts. It leads an aspiring writer to say, "I will write a play on the theme of God Is Not Mocked, or The State versus the Individual, or Racial Intolerance, or Women's Liberation, or The Tragedy of Man's Pursuit of the Unattainable." In fact the theme will take care of itself (and may well turn out to be a very different theme from the one intended), provided the author is sparked off by something; and this something is often a small human incident.

The theme is best inferred from the action, not stated. It is often so deeply embedded in the writer's subconscious that if he were asked to state it, he could only reply that the play had said it all. The play is his statement. This is why so few playwrights, and artists in general, are willing to talk about the "meaning" of their work.

Formulas

Instead of the grand approach to play writing, it might be better to apply a well-tried formula, such as "Get a man up a tree in the first act, throw stones at him in the second, rescue him in the third"; "Boy meets girl, boy loses girl, boy gets girl"; "Sex, class, and religion." It is not a bad idea on a first attempt to observe the classic unities of time, place, and action, though this is certainly a rule made to be broken.

Inspiration

Many writers have found their original inspiration in a small newspaper item that intrigued them, a court case, perhaps, which set them thinking what sort of man the accused was. Or a conversation overheard in a hotel lounge, or a crossed line on the phone, or a sharp exchange in a train compartment before the parties clammed up. Very often it is some experience of their own, perhaps not important, but containing possibilities. Anecdotes ignite a train of thought quicker than themes, and it is better to concentrate on them.

History, biography, psychology, science, and philosophy abound in anecdotes, incidents, and cases that activate creative thought. John Arden, for example, modeled the character of Musgrave in his play *Serjeant Musgrave's Dance* on Oliver Cromwell.

Dramatic Concrete Objects: *Lady Windermere's Fan*___

A concrete object is a better starting point than a universal theme. Oscar Wilde may have wanted to write a play about the hypocrisy of society, but it was the fan Lady Windermere's husband gave her as a birthday present that really captured his imagination. It threads the entire plot together. By the end of the first act, it promises drama for the second. At the ball, when the crucial moment of confrontation comes, Lady Windermere's courage fails her, and she does not strike Mrs. Erlynne with the fan. At the climax of the third act, the fan is discovered in Lord Darlington's rooms and almost causes a duel between him and Lord Windermere. In the fourth act, the fan provides the pretext for Mrs. Erlynne's return and brings about the resolution of the play.

The Silver Box _____

John Galsworthy may have wanted to write a play about crime, punishment, and social justice; but it was the silver box that enabled him to do it. In his play of that title, a rich young man and an unemployed workman steal a purse and a silver cigarette box while drunk. The young man is protected by his father's wealth and influence. The worker is sent to jail.

Examples abound where a dramatic concrete object is central to the plot of a play or a novel: Caesar's will, Desdemona's handkerchief, Raina's photograph in *Arms and the Man*, Henry James's golden bowl. If a playwright is stuck for a subject, he could do worse than turn out his pockets and attempt a play about a ticket stub, a key ring, or a pencil sharpener.

The MacGuffin

The rationale behind Alfred Hitchcock's best comedy film thrillers—the thing that causes the chases, danger, excitement, and suspense—is dubbed by him as "the MacGuffin." We often do not find out until the last reel what the MacGuffin is, and by then it does not really matter. "The MacGuffin," says Hitchcock, "is nothing at all." It is simply an invisible hare that sets the plot in motion and keeps it going until the end.

Much of *North by Northwest* consists of a chase after a man who does not exist. But the true MacGuffin emerges at the very end, when the Soviet spies are caught trying to take a piece of Mexican sculpture containing microfilm out of the country. What does the microfilm show? We do not know or care. What matters is that the MacGuffin is invested with enough importance by the principal characters to create the highly entertaining story we have just witnessed. They should want it so badly they are willing to plot feverishly to get it and to chase after it to the ends of the earth.

Rosebud

It is a bonus of course when the MacGuffin does have significance; for example, the clever device used by Orson Welles and Herman Mankiewicz in *Citizen Kane*. What did the mighty newspaper magnate Charles Foster Kane mean by his dying word "Rosebud"? An investigative reporter (*i.e.*, a detective) spends almost the entire film trying to track down the answer. At the end he still does not know, but in the meantime we have been enthralled by the story of Kane's life, as related by those closest to him. Virtually in the last shot we are let into the secret of Rosebud, and it does suggest a valid reason for Kane's enormous ambition. But its real function is to tell Kane's life story in the form of a difficult quest; in other words, as a suspenseful dramatic action.

Experience

A playwright should write about something that interests him, or it will not interest his audience. This is not to say, "Write only about what you know." If obeyed blindly, this stricture limits invention and imagination.

Playwrights do write about the emotions they know, of course, and a play is very often based on a traumatic experience in the life of the author. But to be successful here, a playwright needs a sense of detachment from that experience. In the artist, said Eliot, there should be a strict separation between the man who suffers and the mind which creates.

Allegory is a useful way to achieve detachment. The emotional roots of Arthur Miller's *The Crucible* are to be found in the author's own experiences during the McCarthy witch hunts. But he wisely set his play in a totally different age, three centuries earlier.

What Makes a Classic

Although it is a bad starting point for composition, a play's theme is ultimately of central importance. It is basically what the play is about, what the writer has to say.

A universal theme which never dates and has meaning for all people is one of the ingredients that confers immortality on a play. Others are vital characters, superb construction, great language, and irresistible parts for actors.

Drama is about man's basic drives for glory, wealth, and power; it is about his basic needs for food, shelter, sex, and occupation; it is about romantic love, jealousy, madness, lives shored up by illusion...family conflicts, rivalries, and hatreds...order in the state moving into chaos then returning to order...crime, tyranny, war, assassination, revolution...boredom.... All these subjects and themes have been with mankind for a long time, and Hamlet's definition of the purpose of drama is still the best—to hold a mirror up to nature. It should satisfy Marxists too, for if nature's reflection is sufficiently cruel, stupid, or complacent and something can be done about it, it will make the audience angry enough to want to change the society that created those conditions.

To fashion a mirror of life and truth is what every dramatist should aspire to. However far below it he may fall, he should strive to create scenes, as Dr. Johnson said of Shakespeare, "from which a hermit may estimate the transactions of the world, and a confessor predict the progress of the passions."

Drama and Politics

The political content of an exciting play or film is often discounted, though it is its mainspring. The political corruption in Chicago in the 1920s is essential for the dramatic success of Hecht and MacArthur's newspaper farce-comedy *The Front Page*. It is the merging of several powerful strands of international politics in a unique place at a very particular time—December 1941, days before America entered World War II—that gives the film *Casablanca* its richness and lasting appeal. *Odd Man Out* is a parable set in the unending Irish troubles. *The Third Man* is steeped in the power politics of post-war Europe. O'Casey's early masterpieces are historical documents.

This should be remembered when it comes to more didactic plays. Characters should not be mere mouthpieces for the author's "message." The dialogue will descend to pamphleteering or the recitation of editorials.

"If you are going to write what is called a propaganda play," said Howard Lindsay, "don't let any character in the play know what the propaganda is." Walter Kerr went a stage further and said that even the playwright should not know what the propaganda is. Sam Goldwyn went too far: "Messages are for Western Union."

Priorities

If an author does have a strong message to get across, he must be a dramatic artist first and a propagandist second. Otherwise his words will be ineffective and will almost certainly bore the audience.

With no political propagandizing whatsoever, *The Voysey Inheritance* is, by implication, one of the most devastating attacks on capitalism ever written.

Matched Forces

A play suffers from being too one-sided; if one viewpoint railroads all opposition, it lacks the vital element of equally matched, contending forces.

Shaw

In *Saint Joan*, Shaw was at pains to give cogent arguments to the Maid's persecutors. He was so determined also that his plays should not become Socialist tracts and should appeal as drama, that the anti-Socialist "villain," such as Undershaft, the armaments manufacturer in *Major Barbara*, often emerged as the hero. Shaw even has Undershaft boasting that the true creed of the armorer is "Nothing is ever done in this world until men are prepared to kill one another if it is not done." (It also suited Shaw's temperament. He enjoyed standing an idea on its head, just as Wilde enjoyed reversing a cliché.)

Look Back in Anger

The important character Colonel Redfern, Jimmy Porter's father-in-law in John Osborne's *Look Back in Anger*, shows the author's unexpected sympathy with the golden age of Empire. The Colonel acts as a strong counter-balance to Jimmy's blasts against the English upper classes and their imperial heritage (though even these tirades contain a certain ambivalence).

Brecht and Mao Tse-tung

Brecht's intentions in *Mother Courage* were the exact opposite of what he achieved. He wanted the audience to see Courage as a rather contemptible figure living off the war, but she has come to personify the indestructibility of the human spirit. The artist in him overcame the didactic propagandist.

Brecht also said, in his recorded conversations, that the primary purpose of theater was to entertain. And Mao Tse-tung, no less, asserted, "Works of art which lack artistic quality have no force, however progressive they are politically."

Dramatic Impact

Plays can indeed be explosive when the social and political content is married to dramatic artistry. A production of *Coriolanus* in Paris in 1934 so enraged both Communists and Fascists that riots broke out. Performances of Greek tragedies were suppressed by the Colonels' regime in Greece as being subversive—2500 years after they were written.

On the night of the massacre in Kazansky Square in 1905, Stanislavsky was acting with the Moscow Art Theatre in Petrograd. Censors sat in on the performance to make sure nothing seditious got through. The cumulative force of the drama began to raise the audience, already inflamed by the events of the day, to a pitch of excitement. When the play's hero came to a stirring passage about truth and freedom, the dam burst. The entire audience rose cheering from their seats and rushed at the stage. Stanislavsky had to shake hundreds of outstretched hands. "That evening," he wrote later, "I found out through my own experience what power the theatre can exercise." But, then, the play was *An Enemy of the People*, Ibsen's masterpiece about the triumph of the individual conscience over the corruption and vested interests of society. A lesser artist would not have exerted that power.

CHARACTERIZATION

9

Characterization and dialogue are areas of drama that cannot be taught, any more than medical science can create human life. But there are useful pointers that can be given.

"Type" Character

It is common practice to decry the "type" character, comparing it unfavorably with the individualized, well-rounded character, realized in psychological depth.

Baker, Archer, and most commentators tend to disdain the "type." The notable exception is Eric Bentley.

There is much value and considerable vitality in the old comedy of humors; in the idea that people are characterized by one ruling passion. The idea has proved richly successful in Molière, the Roman comic dramatists, Ben Jonson, and Shakespeare. Despite the great complexity of Shakespeare's finest creations, there is also a great simplicity and often a very clear single, dominant passion. Greek tragedy is full of characters that are, in fact, single, dominant passions with human identities. An audience will stand up and applaud "a passion" delivered with élan.

Humors and Obsessions

The ancient tradition that there are only four main humors—choler, melancholy, phlegm, and blood—may appear far too simplifed, but, taking a bold view and regarding phlegm as "coldness," can a better description be found for the essential natures of Lear, Hamlet, Iago, and Othello?

The protagonists of Molière—Harpagon, M. Jourdain, or Arnolphe—are, in fact, personified obsessions. The dominant passion is the *idée fixe*, a mind locked frenziedly in a single track, almost to the point of madness.

Genet, in effect, divides humanity into only two types—the dominant and the subservient.

Farce and Melodrama

Many of the stock characters of farce and melodrama have immense vitality. No one could describe Rufus T. Firefly or Otis B. Driftwood as complex characters probed in psychological depth, yet Groucho Marx's wild, bizarre creations have more voltage than many "profound" studies of human nature. For example, in *Monkey Business*:

ANGRY HUSBAND: (*suspecting Groucho is after his wife*): I'm wise. I'm wise.

GROUCHO: You're wise, eh? Well, what's the capital of Nebraska? What's the capital of the Chase National Bank? Give up? Now for an easy one. How many Frenchmen can't be wrong?...

The colorful personages of the *Commedia dell' Arte* have countless offspring in world drama.

Touring companies in Britain and America always had to include a Soubrette, a Low Comedian, an Adventuress, an Old Man, a Juvenile, an Ingenue, and other standard types.

The Pilgrim's Progress

An apprentice playwright is on surer ground if he thinks less about creating complex characters and more about, say, the single-qualitied personages of *The Pilgrim's Progress*; the prototypes of

Menander; Victorian melodrama; the characters of very successful television situation comedy; or even the dwarfs in *Snow White*—the principle is the same.

Even in the psychological realms of Ibsen or the subtleties of Chekhov, there are mistaken assumptions. Chekhov usually has a traditional villain—Soliony, for example—who brings about a tragic turn of events. And, for all her complexities, Hedda Gabler can be viewed as a traditional villainess. Psychologists themselves type-cast people.

Stereotypes

A warning is needed though. The stock character is justified only on the grounds of its vitality. If it does not spring to life, the result is far worse than a careful observation of an unusual person that does not quite make it as valid characterization. We are left with the boring stereotype, the cipher that inhabits so many bad plays, unoriginal, one-dimensional, based on received ideas of what motivates people.

It is also a good idea to avoid a relentless procession of abstractions marching across the stage: Man; the Human Condition; Fate; Virtue; Guilt; the Future; Wisdom.... Invariably, bringing up the rear will be another—Disaster.

The stereotype was condemned by Congreve, who said it required little more than a good memory and superficial observation. A very accurate dissection of nature was needed to portray a true humor, which he defined as "a singular and unavoidable manner of doing or saying anything, peculiar and natural to one man only; by which his speech and actions are distinguished from those of other men." Only talent can reproduce this, and talent is unteachable. A would-be writer has that searching insight into human nature, intuitive grasp of truth, X-ray vision, call it what you will—or he does not.

Individualization

Whatever his method, the playwright seeks to individualize his characters, to differentiate them, so that the audience immediately senses two or more minds interacting.

It must always be a character that speaks, asserted Ben Hecht, the comic dramatist, *not a line born of another line.*

Contrasted Characters

Contrasted characters have already been mentioned as a dramatic device. It is a favorite technique of dramatists. Why is this? Human nature is full of contradictions. They are to be found in everyone, but they are especially marked in the case of the dramatist. Within himself he may find doubt and certainty, cruelty and compassion, commitment to a political philosophy and rebellion against any form of commitment, romantic love and cynical lechery, masculine and feminine elements. He often strives to resolve his internal conflicts and reach the truth in dramatic form. Embodying two extremes in contrasting characters is one way of doing this. Ibsen was both Gregers Werle and Hjalmar Ekdal; Chekhov was both Trigorin and Constantine; Shakespeare was both Othello and Iago.

But the practical reason, in terms of technique, is that the action of the play is strikingly braced by contrasted characters. It becomes more clear-cut and decisive. And the audience is not put into a fog of confusion about who is doing what and why.

Examples

Hamlet

Hamlet is contrasted with conventional men of action—Fortinbras and Laertes—and also with his best friend. The Prince's wild exultant delight at the success of his play is countered by a laconic Horatio who sees that his manic mood is dangerous. Hamlet improvises a few lines of doggerel to prove he would make a player:

HORATIO: You might have rhymed.
HAMLET: O good Horatio, I'll take the ghost's word for a thousand pound. Didst perceive?
HORATIO: Very well, my lord.
HAMLET: Upon the talk of the poisoning—
HORATIO: I did very well note him.

Othello

Two very different women in *Othello* are defined by their contrasting attitudes to sex. Desdemona can hardly credit that some wives are unfaithful to their husbands.

DESDEMONA: Wouldst thou do such a deed for all the world?
EMILIA: Why, would not you?
DESDEMONA: No, by this heavenly light!
EMILIA: Nor I neither by this heavenly light:
               I might do't as well i' th' dark.

Endless Combinations

None of the foregoing denies the immense range of human character and temperament, and the endless combinations of its component powers and defects, inclinations and aversions that individualize men, nor how an individual can be torn by contending emotions.

No man or woman's character is fixed and immutable, which is antagonistic to the nature of drama. As we have seen, a character can change considerably from act to act and, indeed, before our very eyes. A good play is alive from minute to minute; it is in a continual state of flux. It cannot stand still; nor the characters in it. The tension of ambiguity will operate, too. Contradictory elements can exist in the same character and be held together at one instant. Turn the prism, and he or she is a different person.

A National Theatre production note on the paradox of *The Misanthrope*: A radical says Alceste is a satirist; a conservative says Alceste is the subject of Molière's satire.

action before character; what a character does defines him

Public and Private

A character's behavior will often change with the numbers of people present. Soliony in Chekhov's *Three Sisters* is agreeable to Baron Tusenbach in private but admits he becomes insulting in company. Cordelia's refusal in *King Lear* to profess her undivided love for her father has drastic consequences mainly because it is such a public occasion.

A man's conduct can also be affected by the nature of those present. An ambitious young officer is more likely to take medal-winning risks on the battlefield if he knows he is within range of his general's binoculars. A man will probably be on his best behavior in the presence of the woman he loves; if he is a perverse character, he will be at his worst. Schoolchildren will often be different people with their parents, their teachers, their friends. A hen-pecked husband can be a tyrant at work, and vice versa. The dramatist will deploy his characters on stage to underscore any such changes.

A splendid historical example was Lloyd George who, with chameleon wizardry, absorbed the personality of anyone he was with and, in effect, *became* them. One of his enemies was asked what he was like when he was in a room alone. The reply was: "When Lloyd George is in a room alone, the room is empty."

Unveiling

Instead of a working distinction between the Type and the Individual, it is probably better to distinguish between the character who is all there from the word go—he leaps out at you—and the character who is slowly revealed.

At the heart of much character creation is the idea of development. Archer had a better word for it: "unveiling." The crisis of the play may produce a visible alteration in the protagonist's character, but this is really a supreme manifestation of character, revealing something that was present all along but hidden to the audience. A drama, says Archer, should bring out character as a photographer's chemicals develop a negative. There, literally, is the ideal use of the word "development" when applied to characterization. The character has many layers and only gradually discloses his identity. We do not see him whole until the play is complete. The process again constitutes *action*.

To paraphrase Ibsen: We know the characters at first as we would strangers on a train, then after spending a month's holiday with them, finally after a long and close acquaintance.

Kenneth Tynan insisted that a play's characters should be driven to a state of desperation.

Other Sides

What the process often reveals are the redeeming features of knaves or fools and the unpleasant side of good characters. A supposedly weak character will rise to the occasion. A four-letter man may, at the play's climax, be the only character with enough strength and courage to deal with a fatal emergency. In Boucicault's *London Assurance*, Sir Harcourt Courtly is assumed by the characters and audience to be fop and a coward, but he startles all by accepting the challenge to a duel.

Crampton in *You Never Can Tell* is painted in very harsh colors by his family, and Shaw for a time appears to concur with this view, until M'Comas's long speech in his defense in the third act. After this we understand and sympathize with Crampton much more. George Booth in *The Voysey Inheritance* is a jovial, pleasant old fellow when things are going well, a great friend of the family; but when he learns what the firm has done to his money, he becomes darkly vengeful, a man of spite.

The principle of balance and perspective in characterization, "roundness," if you like, is again related to the idea of two opposing forces held in a state of tension—one of the basic tenets of action and suspense.

Audience Reaction

> Aeschylus, Sophocles, and Euripides did not create the laws of dramatic construction, since those laws exist in the passions and the sympathies of the human race. (Bronson Howard, late nineteenth-century American dramatist.)

An audience must respond positively to the characters in a play—react with feeling, not be indifferent to them. The responses can be wide-ranging—love, hate, compassion, fear, admiration, derision, fascination, curiosity. So, in a melodrama, the audience cheers the hero, hisses the villain, and swoons over the heroine.

Empathy

Empathy on the part of the audience is essential for successful characterization. We must feel with the protagonist if not for him. We must understand to some extent what motivates him. We must know crucial facts about him. Sympathy is not essential, but it can grow out of understanding. Macbeth, Richard III, Hedda Gabler, and Rebecca West are not likeable characters. But, by the end of the play we know them, we have merged our own existence in theirs, we have shared their climactic life experience. We feel compassion for them, and in a way, yes, we even sympathize with them.

How does a playwright involve his audience thus in the fate of his characters?

The strength of feeling in the audience is usually equal to that evidenced on stage—and the strength of feeling there is usually determined by how strongly the driver wants to achieve his goal. We share his inner turbulence, we are caught up in what he is striving to do, we are infected by his passion. We appreciate his forceful self-awareness, his sense of identity. He might paraphrase Descartes, "I want; therefore I am."

Sympathy

If we the audience think he deserves what he wants so badly, if his desire is just, natural, and human, then we take his part completely; we are hopeful when it looks as though he will get what he longs for, fearful when not. This is about as near to a definition of "sympathy" for a character as we are likely to achieve. It is certainly not a question of goodies and baddies. You can have dislikeable worthies and likeable rogues. (These observations, of course, apply also where the play's protagonist is a woman.)

Identification

There are simple fun identifications where the hero is a projection of a man's fantasies. The theatrical experience can be therapeutic: problems in one's own life can be exchanged for those of characters in the play. There is the fearful identification—"There but for the grace of God go I." Or the stage can be a comic mirror where each member of the audience sees everyone reflected except himself.

But the process is really a mystery. We know what it is to be shaken to the core by a dramatic experience, drained of all emotion. The Aristotelian catharsis has it that we are "purged by pity and terror." But no one can say how it is done.

Lessing

The playwright's need, wrote Lessing, is "to transfer himself from the viewpoint of a narrator into the real standpoint of each personage; to let passions arise before the eyes of the audience instead of simply describing them; and to let them grow up without effort in such illusory continuity that the spectator must sympathize, whether he will or no." In the final analysis this cannot be taught. It is inborn.

Character in Action

Character is best revealed through illustrative action. If we are shown some revealing incident, it will pin that character down more surely than any amount of laborious description. James Tyrone's meanness in *Long Day's Journey into Night* is emphasized by his turning out most of the electric lights in the house.

In *The Barretts of Wimpole Street*, Barrett's tyranny is soon established when he forces his favorite daughter Elizabeth to drink a tankard of porter to help her invalid condition. In *You Never Can Tell*, Bohun orders people not to interrupt, but constantly interrupts people himself.

Falstaff's character is instantly caught on his first appearance (*Henry IV* Pt. One. Act I, Scene 2), when he rouses himself after a heavy bout of drinking and asks Prince Hal what time of day it is. One stage tradition has the Prince catching him asleep on a bench.

It is a Hollywood maxim that the villain in a Western should be identified on his first appearance by having him kick a dog.

The character of Felix in Neil Simon's *The Odd Couple*, which is about two men who have broken up with their wives and are sharing an apartment, is illustrated by the wifely role he adopts. He is extremely house proud, cooks proper meals, demands regular hours, and prepares sandwiches of fastidious delicacy for the poker group.

The Princess's neurotic, imperious personality is immediately evidenced in Tennessee Williams' *Sweet Bird of Youth*, when she emerges from her coma and wildly demands her oxygen mask, pills, and vodka.

Stanley Kowalski's boorishness in *A Streetcar Named Desire* is shown in many ways but notably in the way he treats property—throwing the radio out of the window, hurling Blanche's furs about, smashing the supper plates. The gentle Mitch, who has been kind to Blanche, turns cruel when Stanley gives him proof of her wild promiscuity. The action which best illustrates this is when, in order to get a proper look at her, he rips the paper lantern off the light bulb so that the harsh light can shine directly down on her ageing face.

Deference

Character is often illustrated by the deference—or lack of it—paid to each character by the personages. Falstaff, for all his jocularity, has a fundamental deference to Prince Hal, compared with Hal's habitual disrespect toward him.

As already shown, in *Who's Afraid of Virginia Woolf?* Edward Albee early establishes George's and Martha's characters by the contempt with which she treats him and his failure to be stung by this (until he is pushed beyond endurance).

Consistency and Tone

If someone in a play speaks or acts grossly out of character, it destroys plausibility. This is not to stipulate absolute consistency of character, which can cramp a writer and spell death to many an original and challenging interpretation by an actor. But if an audience is confused and irritated and bored by a blatant inconsistency, that can only be counted as a serious loss. There are, of course, capricious characters who are in the habit of acting inconsistently, in which case the playwright should establish this early.

The principle applies to the tone of a play as a whole. It should not switch jarringly from one form of drama to another. Ibsen's early play *The League of Youth*, for example, begins as a telling political satire, then lurches wildly into a farce about philandering.

Likes and Dislikes

Strong opinions, likes and dislikes define a character, but they must be realized in action if that character is to move the play forward.

If it is the author's intention to portray a hypocrite, of course, his opinions will be shown to be hollow.

A character's whole set of values can, in fact, be conveyed by one or two remarks; for example, the waiter in *You Never Can Tell* (see excerpt on page 97).

Parodies

Once the behavior of characters is established and their speech patterns known, it is possible to predict how the *dramatis personae* would react in all kinds of situations. Composing parodies can be a useful play writing exercise. So, just for fun, consider the tragic quartet of Eugene O'Neill's *Long Day's Journey into Night*, based very closely on the bitter feuds within his own family: the famed American actor James O'Neill, too mean to get his son Eugene, the future dramatist, cured of tuberculosis; the drunken playboy brother; the morphine-addicted mother. How would they regard Eugene, now that he has joined them across the Great Divide? In Elysium, the scene of my burlesque, nothing would have changed.

Eugene's Pay-Off

EUGENE: We are the fog people...
JAMES O'NEILL: Let's have none of that morbid, decadent talk. There's no fog here, lad. It's eternal sunlight in God's blessed fields.
EUGENE: That should save you something in electric light bills.
JAMES O'NEILL: Oh I could see that poisonous crack coming! You turned me into a fine boozy ham actor and tightwad for my Lord Laurence Olivier to make a mockery of. But Edwin Booth told me only the other day that I played Othello better than Laurence Olivier ever did. His very words.
EUGENE: Father, I wrote that play out of love and pity for you.
JAMES O'NEILL: That's a lie! You did it to make capital out of our sufferings. And you lied I was sending you to die in a cheap sanatorium, when you lived another forty years and won great riches and glory. Thank God I've kept it from your mother. They've given her the cold turkey treatment here. If she ever got to read your play she'd go right back on the needle again.

(*Enter Eugene's elder brother*, JAMIE, *stinking drunk*)

JAMIE:	Cheer up, kid. I love your guts. Pass the booze. You wrote some harsh things about us. But I know you never meant it. That's why I gave Mother a copy of *Long Day's Journey into Night* as a fun birthday present.

(EUGENE *and* JAMES SENIOR *rise in horror*)

EUGENE:	Jamie, you bastard!
JAMIE:	You were right, kid. I *do* hate your guts. Now Mother will know who's the real louse in the family!

(*Enter* MRS. ELLA QUINLAN O'NEILL, *glassy-eyed, stoned on morphine*)

MRS. O'NEILL:	The Archangels were so kind to me yesterday...
JAMIE:	"I wandered lonely as a cloud..."
MRS. O'NEILL:	I told them all things seemed to stretch forward in time-less serenity.... Then something horrible happened. Yes, I remember now. I was given a copy of a play written by my son, Eugene...

(JAMES SENIOR *looks in black fury at* EUGENE. JAMIE *gloats.* EUGENE *hangs his head in shame*).

Adequate Motivation

A character's motivation should be adequate and logical. Inade-quate motivation occurs when the conduct of the people in the play does not seem to grow out of their characters. They are the creatures of any situation into which the dramatist wishes to thrust them.

In a good play it is the characters who generate the action. They have a life and a will of their own. But, all too often in in-ferior work, the author pushes them on and takes them off when he wants, moves them to places he wants them to be, shoves them into conflicts, and forces the conclusion that he, the puppet-master, desires. And that is the way the characters come across—as puppets, not living people. Oedipus drives himself into the abyss. Sophocles does not order him there.

A good writer finding himself in a "block" where his dramatic situation will not work knows it is almost certainly because he is forcing his characters. He stops, looks at them more closely, im-agines their past history, and invents new characters. His problem often eases with new reasons for action. Situations are born out of character. Indeed, Galsworthy said, "Character is situation."

Explanations

Explanations for a character's conduct need to be skillfully deployed.

Richard III's crooked and deformed body is certainly one plausible reason for his lust after power and majesty. It is significant that Hedda Gabler's father was a general. It accounts to some extent for her contempt for Tesman. She has married beneath her socially, and Tesman is clearly her father's inferior in character. The same applies in *Who's Afraid of Virginia Woolf?* where Martha's father, whom she reveres, is president of the university and much more successful than her husband, George. In Chekhov's *Three Sisters*, Soliony's self-identification with the romantic poet Lermontov, who was killed in a duel, helps explain why he will tolerate no rival for Irina, and at the play's end kills Tusenbach in a duel.

Glib Motivations

There is a contrasting danger of glib, or hyper-analytical motivation.

All too often a character's "motives" are grafted onto the body of the play as an extraneous commentary or explanation by the author, sometimes unrelated to anything we have seen the character do.

As mentioned, too much importance, even in the greatest drama, can be attached to the motives of characters, as if the fact that they are tremendously alive were not in itself sufficient.

Lear

Why is King Lear choleric, tyrannical, and obsessed with his daughters? It is enough that he is so. It would doubtless be convenient for some if Shakespeare had inserted a speech stating that Lear's dead Queen had been unfaithful to him, and that Cordelia was the only child he knew for certain was his own. But he did not.

Who cares about Jimmy Porter's motives, or lack of them, in John Osborne's *Look Back in Anger*? The point is that he is extremely vibrant and funny.

Iago

Volumes have been written about Iago's motives. Even Shakespeare supplies him with three or four (see pp. 90–91). But any audience, given a good performance, will not worry unduly. They simply recognize Iago as one of nature's destroyers.

Hamlet

It is eternally asked, "Why did Hamlet delay?" "Was he mad?" But why should he *not* delay? Tom Stoppard satirizes the theorists in *Rosencrantz and Guildenstern are Dead*:

> To sum up: your father, whom you love, dies, you are his heir, you come back to find that hardly was the corpse cold before his young brother popped on to his throne and into his sheets, thereby offending both legal and natural practice. Now why exactly are you behaving in this extraordinary manner?

Dynamic Motivation

Genuine motivation is built into the action. The audience, for example, may see something happen in Act One that creates a strong motive for events in Act Three.

Proctor's guilt because of his adultery with Abigail in *The Crucible* directly affects the way he behaves in the court hearing at the play's climax.

The Master Builder

In Ibsen's *The Master Builder*, Hilde Wangel's first encounter with Solness, ten years before the play begins, when she was only thirteen, is a vital motivating force throughout the drama. She had nearly caused the great builder to fall off his church tower by waving and screaming with excitement as he placed a wreath on top of it; and his flirtation with her later that day was clearly for her a sexual awakening. In the first act she arrives as an alluring young temptress of twenty-three to claim the "kingdom" he promised her. She soon becomes his driving demon. At the play's end, Solness falls to his death from the spire of his last building which she has challenged him to climb.

Rosmersholm

In Ibsen's *Rosmersholm*, Rebecca West's motivations are complex, but it convincingly emerges that, because she succeeded one woman (her mother) with Dr. West, she was impelled to repeat the process with Rosmer, driving his wife, Beata, to suicide.

Concealed Motives

The concealment of motives—one cloaking another, where characters may deceive themselves as well as others—is good dramatic material, whether in tragedy or comedy, particularly when the truth is finally sprung. Jealousy and spite masquerading as moral indignation; a marked concern for a woman's reputation and safety that conceals a sexual interest in her; an obsession with the fine print of a political party's constitution, masking a power struggle for the leadership; a fierce puritanical zeal that has its roots in sexual repression; a psychopath or emotional cripple finding an outlet and justification for his murderous impulses in political extremism.

The Probable Impossibility

An audience will swallow far more at the beginning of a play than it will later on. It will accept an absurd premise in the first fifteen minutes, provided it is worked through logically. The first scene of *King Lear* is not very credible, but this does not bother an audience. From then on the play has a ruthless logic and inevitability. Lear's rage against Cordelia may not be plausible, but it makes entirely plausible his rage against Goneril and Regan later. And if anyone, having read the play completely through, goes straight back to the first scene, it will then seem far more plausible. Once we know him, that sudden violent rejection of one so dear to him is just the sort of thing Lear would do.

There are few more absurd premises in drama than that of *Oedipus Rex*. The American writer and cartoonist Jules Feiffer once showed the blinded Oedipus in black glasses telling his analyst, "You should talk to my daughter. Boy, has *she* got problems." (Is not Antigone her own aunt?) But the logic of the play is fireproof. It is like a scientific proposition that says, "Given such and such, the chain of consequences will be thus and thus." And it will inevitably be so.

Aristotle put it in the form of a paradox: "A probable impossibility is preferable to an improbable possibility." If a strange thing has actually happened, that is not enough to make an audience buy it. But a dramatist can make an audience accept something never likely to happen, provided he works through his premise logically. Ghost stories, fairy tales, animal stories, and science fiction all confirm the point.

Coincidence

Far-fetched coincidences are to be avoided, but they too can work if introduced early. It is an incredible coincidence that Elyot and Amanda in Coward's *Private Lives* should find themselves in adjoining balcony rooms on their second honeymoons. The audience accepts it, however, because it comes at the start of the play.

Deus ex Machina

A *deus ex machina*, the intervention of divine providence or an authoritarian figure who disentangles the plot when the author himself cannot do it, has little to recommend it. Even the greatest dramatists are not free from the fault, for example, in Molière's *Tartuffe*, where Louis XIV sorts everything out at the end of the play.

Entrances and Exits

The playwright watches the practical difficulties of getting his characters on and off. Entrances and exits should be logical, in character, and well motivated. O'Neill (to be serious) manages this skillfully in *Long Day's Journey*. He brings about permutations of dialogue between the four members of the Tyrone family, involving confidences the others are not allowed to hear.

Entrances and exits often denote character: the patsy in a Neil Simon or Ayckbourn farce who blunders in at precisely the wrong moment; the calm, collected first entrance of a dangerous man and the silence he produces—Dick Dudgeon in the first act of Shaw's *The Devil's Disciple*; the final exit of the humiliated Malvolio in

Twelfth Night, snarling, "I'll be revenged on the whole pack of you!" Sheridan Whiteside is wheeled in by the nurse in *The Man Who Came to Dinner*, and, not one to mince words, his first line in the play is "I may vomit."

Characters Talking About Each Other

A character talking about himself or herself; two characters talking about each other; two characters talking about a third who is not present—these are inferior to illustrative action, but they can be skillfully employed.

Self-exposition is very common in Chekhov, and it works because of the amusing contrast between the character's total immersion in himself and the indifference of the company around him. But generally it should be avoided. As Baker says, "When a character stands outside itself, describing what it feels, the speaker is really the author in disguise, describing what he is incompetent, from lack of sympathetic power, to phrase with simple, moving accuracy." It is often better for the playwright to show the symptoms of a passion and to let the audience make its own diagnosis.

Characters talking about others offstage *can* be effective, because at the same time the speaker defines himself, as Cassius does when he vilifies Caesar. When Portia or Célimène talk scathingly of their suitors, they summon up graphic portraits of the characters being assassinated and, at the same time, illustrate the caustic wit of their own natures. The characters in *Hedda Gabler* define themselves while talking about Loevborg.

Iago's First Diatribe

While remembering that one character's opinion of another is not necessarily the dramatist's, Iago's first major speech in the opening scene of *Othello* is an impressive example. It defines himself, Othello, and Cassio. He exhibits his own jealous vindictive fury that he, a combat soldier, has been passed over by Othello, who has chosen a smooth staff officer, Cassio, to be his lieutenant. It seems Iago is a person of some consequence because "three great ones of the city" petitioned Othello on his behalf, though without success. (He may be lying, of course, but at this stage of the play we have no reason to doubt him.)

Iago defines Othello as bombastic, "horribly stuffed with epithets of war" (no bad description) and mimics him, a clever device by which a character on stage can bring one absent to life: "'Certes,' says he, 'I have already chose my officer.'" (In the National Theatre production of 1964 Frank Finlay here slipped into an imitation of Olivier.) Iago also defines Cassio who is "almost damned in a fair wife" (a hint of the plot to come), and who "never set a squadron in the field, Nor the division of a battle knows More than a spinster." On the other hand he, Iago, has proved himself on several fields of battle. Indirectly the speech also defines Roderigo, to whom it is addressed—the gullible sidekick, hanging on his master's utterances, who has his own reasons for hating Othello. (*Note*: The speech has divided great Shakespearean critics. Bradley in effect says it is all lies, Granville Barker believes that Shakespeare intended us to take it substantially at its face value. What is undeniable is that Iago drives the play off with force, providing us rapidly with sharp characterizations of the chief male actors in the tragedy.)

Emphasis

The technique is also important for emphasis. Shakespeare does not allow us to forget Hamlet when he is offstage, because the other characters keep talking about him.

It is generally a good idea to delay the appearance of the central character, and prepare the way for his entrance with a certain amount of discussion about him.

Talk about characters who never appear can be vivid, as John Osborne proved in *Look Back in Anger*; and in *The Hotel in Amsterdam*, the all-pervasive hero "KL" was never seen.

Pitfalls

However, characters talking about other characters offstage or to their face can go badly wrong. A common result is that a man will listen to theories about his character placed in the mouths of other characters by the playwright. Pamela in Osborne's *Time Present* says about such plays, "People sit around and make up Freudian epigrams about one another. It's written by someone thinking about writing it, instead of thinking about whatever it is about."

It cannot be emphasized too strongly that the best way to show character is by illustrative action.

Economy

The display of character has to be kept within very strict limits in drama. Much excellent portrayal of character, which the novel has time for, is prevented in a play by the demands of plot, dialogue, subject matter, and the play's length of performance. The number of lines any character has to say is limited to what bears on the play as a whole and advances the action.

Ibsen is especially remarkable for the tautness and economy of his construction. There is hardly a single superfluous line in *Hedda Gabler*. Each one illuminates character and advances the action. Indeed, the distinction between plot and character becomes invisible in any really good play.

Superfluous characters should be cut out. A good playwright compacts as much as possible. If two or even three characters can be compressed into one, it makes his play that much tighter. And he will certainly earn the thanks of actors who dislike coming on for one or two lines only. Cameo parts must be essential to the plot.

Relationships

Characters do not exist in isolation. They reveal themselves in relationships. It is the effect they have on each other, the way they interact, influence, change each other, and the whole course of the action, that count.

ANTONY:	You'll heat my blood: no more!
CLEOPATRA:	You can do better yet; but this is meetly.
ANTONY:	Now by my sword—
CLEOPATRA:	And target. Still he mends. But this is not the best. Look, prithee, Charmian, How this Herculean Roman does become The carriage of his chafe.
ANTONY:	I'll leave you, lady.
CLEOPATRA:	Courteous lord, one word...

Bending the Mind

The most potent Shakespearean image is not really one of conflict, but of a mouth whispering urgently into an ear—someone being "got at." Brutus and Cassius; Macbeth and Lady Macbeth; Othello and Iago; Coriolanus and Volumnia.

BRUTUS: What means this shouting? I do fear the people
Choose Caesar for their king.

CASSIUS: Ay, do you fear it?
Then must I think you would not have it so.

BRUTUS: I would not, Cassius; yet I love him well.
But wherefore do you hold me here so long?

MACBETH: If we should fail,—

LADY MACBETH: We fail!
But screw your courage to the sticking-place,
And we'll not fail.

Perhaps Hamlet's real tragedy was to be urged on only by a ghost. After it vanished, he was left alone and incapable of decisive action.

Obstacles to Love

It is worth noting that the most memorable love relationships in plays are not those of mutual adoration (which translates dully to the stage) but sexual antagonism: Beatrice and Benedick in *Much Ado About Nothing*; Mirabell and Millamant in *The Way of the World*; Célimène and Alceste in *The Misanthrope*; John Tanner and Ann Whitefield in Shaw's *Man and Superman*; Elyot and Amanda in Coward's *Private Lives*; George and Martha in *Who's Afraid of Virginia Woolf?*; films like *The Owl and the Pussycat* and *A Touch of Class*. And, of course, Petruchio and Kate in *The Shrew*.

The attraction expresses itself through hostility. The obstacles do not need to come from outside. They are grounded in the personalities of the protagonists. As a result, their dialogue has more wit, sprightliness, and entertainment value than the cooing of two love birds. "I love you"; "I love you too" is not very promising dialogue. The parties are too much in agreement.

In order to make a traditional romance work in drama there

must be an obstacle. In fact, the more in tune the partners are, the greater the external obstacle needs to be. Romeo and Juliet are star-crossed. Even their most famous love scene contains an obstacle—the balcony. Barrett is the obstacle to Elizabeth and Robert Browning's happiness. A gulf of two centuries separates the lovers in the time play *Berkeley Square*. In the classic weepie *Random Harvest*, the obstacle is the hero's amnesia.

As far as drama is concerned, the course must indeed never run smooth. The audience must ask, Will love conquer all? Will boy get girl?

Waste

The operation of suspense line by line in a love scene is well illustrated in Granville Barker's *Waste*, written in 1906, but very modern in its attitudes. The question is, will Henry Trebell and Mrs. Amy O'Connell, who are both guests at a weekend house party, go to bed together? They tease and maneuver, but neither really knows the answer. They are attracted, but Amy's fears and Trebell's cold-blooded approach are the obstacles.

AMY: I don't want to tempt you. Yes, I do. But you don't look one bit...even now...as if you were in love with me. Yes, you do...yes, you do. But you've not said you love me. Why don't you say so?

TREBELL: I'll say whatever's necessary.

AMY: Don't gibe! I hate you when you gibe. Not even asked me if I love you!

TREBELL: Don't you? Do you? Don't you?

AMY: We don't mean the same thing by it, I'm afraid.

TREBELL: It comes to the same thing.

AMY: Henry...you have a coarse mind! No...
I'll have nothing to do with you.

TREBELL: Very well.

AMY: I won't be played with...

DIALOGUE

10

The primary purpose of good dramatic dialogue is to state clearly the facts that advance the action of the play. Its basic form is to be found in the Latin mass or catechism—a simple statement and response, or a question-and-answer technique.

The form has been and still is used to great effect by the *Commedia dell' Arte*, Molière, court-room dramas, detective stories, stand-up comedians.

Dialogue should grow out of a previous speech or action and lead into another. It is like a good scene sequence. Usually there is some momentary point of rest, a way-station that a particular passage of dialogue was making toward. Then it kicks forward again.

Mourning Becomes Electra

The first part of Eugene O'Neill's *Mourning Becomes Electra* has the following passage where townspeople and workers on the Mannon estate see Christine come out on the steps of the house:

MINNIE:	My! She's awful handsome, ain't she?
LOUISA:	Too furrin lookin' fur my taste.
MINNIE:	Ayeh. There's somethin' queer-lookin' about her face.
AMES:	Secret lookin'—'s if it was a mask she'd put on. That's the Mannon look. They all has it. They grow it on their wives. Seth's growed it on too, didn't you notice—from bein' with 'em all his life. They don't want folks to guess their secrets.
MINNIE:	Secrets?
LOUISA:	The Mannons got skeletons in their closets same as others! Worse ones. (*whispers to* AMES) Tell Minnie about old Abe Mannon's brother David marryin' that French Canuck nurse girl he'd got into trouble.
AMES:	Ssshh! Shut it, can't you? Here's Seth comin'.

The point that O'Neill wants to make is the scandal about the Mannon brother and the French Canadian nurse. Having reached it, he cuts off suddenly, changes tack in order to whet curiosity. But the passage is still directed naturally, and in character, toward that end, starting with the simple comment that Christine is a handsome woman. The operative words which form an associative chain are "handsome," "foreign-looking," "queer-looking," "secret-looking," "secrets," "skeletons," and then the fact about the scandal. One line leads to another and advances the scene. The expository point advances the action.

The lines of the dialogue should be in character and express the character's mood. As stressed before, it must always be a person that speaks, not the mere shadow or echo of the preceding line.

You Never Can Tell

Here is an extract from the embarrassing family reunion at lunch in the second act of Shaw's *You Never Can Tell*.

DOLLY:	Is your son a waiter, too, William?
WAITER:	(*serving* GLORIA *with fowl*): Oh no, miss: he's too impetuous. He's at the Bar.
M'COMAS:	(*patronizingly*): A potman, eh?
WAITER:	(*with a touch of melancholy, as if recalling a disappointment softened by time*): No sir: the other bar. Your profession, sir. A QC sir.

M'COMAS: (*embarrassed*): I'm sure I beg your pardon.

WAITER: Not at all, sir. Very natural mistake, I'm sure sir. I've often wished he was a potman, sir. Would have been off my hands ever so much sooner, sir. (*Aside to* VALENTINE, *who is again in difficulties*) Salt at your elbow, sir. (*Resuming*) Yes, sir: had to support him until he was thirty-seven, sir. But doing well now, sir: very satisfactory indeed, sir. Nothing less than fifty guineas, sir.

It is a characteristic of young Dolly Clandon that she asks pert questions. It is one of the things that brings her to life as a character. It also makes her a natural asset to the play's exposition. The waiter answers her question, and Dolly does not speak again here. She has served Shaw's purpose, which is to introduce the subject of the son's job. There is now a small gear change in the dialogue.

M'Comas, the family solicitor, misinterprets the word "Bar." Shaw engineers this for several reasons. He wants to illustrate M'Comas's character—jumping to wrong conclusions, the condescension, then the embarrassment. He also wants to illustrate the character of the waiter, who has a notably contrasting set of values, takes no offense whatever, but is sensitive to M'Comas's embarrassment and skillfully eases it. The mistake also leads to the emphasis of a significant point. The waiter's gentle revelation that his son is a QC is stronger for coming in the form of a contradiction.

The subject might then be closed, but Shaw wants it kept open. M'Comas keeps it open for him by apologizing. The waiter is kind to him—"I've often wished he was a potman, sir" (true)—but then has to explain why. This leads to further information Shaw wishes to impart about the QC son, who is to become the dominant character of the play's final act. We already know he is "impetuous." The fact that the waiter had to support his son until he was thirty-seven (which is almost what Shaw's mother did with Shaw) is amusing, but in the context of the play as a whole, which has some important things to say about parental and filial duties, it does have a serious purpose.

"Salt at your elbow, sir" again illustrates the waiter's character—his antennae are alive to everything going on about him. The sentences of dramatic dialogue do not have to be grammatically complete. There is no "He" before "would have been..." There is no "He earns" before "nothing less..." This is the way people talk in life. The speech patterns of the waiter are also characteristics that endow him with life. His way of ending every sentence with "sir," his fondness for "very" and "indeed." It gives a gentle rhythm to his speech that is uniquely his own.

Emotionalized Speech _____

Dramatic dialogue consists in the main of emotionalized speech. The facts by themselves are generally colorless. Feeling must be present in the writing for it to reach out to the audience and involve them in the action. In the above example from O'Neill, fear and awe can be sensed in the characters' voices.

The highest flights of dramatic speech are so charged with emotion that the audience is conscious only of blasts of passion. The actual words become jets of fire.

There are inevitable exceptions. Communication of facts in a dry, unemotional way—for example, a surgeon spelling out to a man that he has inoperable cancer—can be very dramatic.

It may help toward variety and contrast of mood in play writing to recall the extent and variety of human feeling. Spinoza lists forty-eight different emotions in his Ethics. Critical gibes like Dorothy Parker's "She ran the whole gamut of her emotions from A to B" may well not be the fault of the actors at all. The playwright never gave them the chance to show what they could do.

> The playwright has to find the buried river of the emotions and then work as an engineer, damming it here, deflecting it there, but always making the fullest use of its natural power. (Eric Bentley)

Link Words _____

Dramatic dialogue can create a skillful cats-cradle of words that keeps a play in motion. In Congreve's *The Way of the World*, Mirabell and Millamant often pick up each other's words in an easy, graceful exhibition of verbal fencing. At one point in the second act, for example, Millamant holds up to scorn, as though with a pair of silver tongs, Mirabell's phrase "beauty is the lover's gift."

Link words can have a devastating dramatic impact in certain contexts, for example, when Iago plants a vague suspicion about Cassio in Othello's mind (Act III, Scene 3).

IAGO:	I did not think he had been acquainted with her.
OTHELLO:	O yes, and went between us very oft.
IAGO:	Indeed!
OTHELLO:	Indeed? Ay, indeed. Discern'st thou aught in that? Is he not honest?
IAGO:	Honest, my lord?
OTHELLO:	Honest! Ay, honest.
IAGO:	My lord, for aught I know.
OTHELLO:	What dost thou think?
IAGO:	Think, my lord?
OTHELLO:	Think, my lord! By heaven, he echoes me, As if there were some monster in his thought Too hideous to be shown...

Again, the emotional coloration of the words, the subtle tones and inflections they invite from the actors, the dangerous undercurrents, and the action within the silences illustrate the nature of true dramatic dialogue. Iago's words fall like drops of poison into a clear fluid, precipitating deadly green flakes.

Misuse

The use of link-words and dialogue hooks can, however, be overdone. See, for example, the following illustration I have invented:

FIONA:	Typical! I should have listened to Mummy before we married. She said you had an unedifying personality.
DERMOT:	*I* have an unedifying personality! She can talk. Evil old toad.
FIONA:	Evil old toad! That's disgusting. If Daddy heard you say that, he'd..he'd horsewhip you.
DERMOT:	Horsewhip me! When he can stand up—he's always blotto.
FIONA:	*He's* always blotto! Look at you and your quarts of pink gin.
DERMOT:	Quarts of pink gin!

(*Enter* RODNEY PERIVALE)

RODNEY: I say, anyone for tennis?

DERMOT: ⎫
FIONA: ⎭ Tennis!!

Weaving Dialogue

Long passages of dialogue should not have a mathematical progression, any more than the plot should. Percival Wilde observes that the novice has a dialogue pattern that goes A B C D E F G H. . . . The experienced writer of dialogue never exhausts a topic as he goes along. He makes a point, leaves it, comes back to it later, leaves it again incomplete, but returns again, each time etching it in deeper. So the progression might be A B C A D B E A C F B G. . . . One comparison is music, where a theme may be introduced, repeated, disappear for a time, and then return at a climactic point with added force.

Challenge and Response

Challenge and response in dialogue are eventually needed for movement. In total agreement—for example, "Quite right, Socrates"; "You've hit the nail on the head there"; "You can say that again, Socrates" (which he does), there is no movement. So, in the first three pages of *King Lear* there is no movement because Goneril and Regan tell the King what he wants to hear. But when Cordelia stubbornly answers: "Nothing," there is a dreadful silence, the King's anger begins to stir—and so does the play.

LEAR: . . .what can you say to draw
           A third more opulent than your sisters? Speak.
CORDELIA: Nothing, my lord.
LEAR: Nothing?
CORDELIA: Nothing.
LEAR: Nothing will come of nothing: speak again.

The word "no" is essential if dialogue is to create movement. It establishes contending forces. It constitutes an obstacle, which invites retaliation.

The basic principles of action and suspense apply in any good passage of dramatic dialogue.

Duologue Dangers

Dialogue can fall too much into duologue. An endless succession of duologues makes for monotony, a fault even the greatest dramatists are not free from, especially in their early work. Ibsen generally compensates for it by his immense underlying tensions. But it is well for inexperienced playwrights to remember the complex dramatic tensions that can be achieved with three, four, or five main characters on stage at once.

The Third Actor

The dramatic possibilities of three actors were first explored by Sophocles. His master scene in this respect occurs in *Oedipus Rex*, when Oedipus and his Queen, Jocasta, make opposite deductions from what the Corinthian messenger says. So much is happening in the scene. It has a terrible dramatic irony.

(JOCASTA *present throughout*)

MESSENGER: That story of pollution through your parents?
OEDIPUS: Ay, that, sir; that, my ever-present torment.
MESSENGER: All idle, sir; your fears are groundless, vain.
OEDIPUS: How can that be, seeing I am their son?
MESSENGER: No. Polybus is no kin of yours.
OEDIPUS: No kin?
Polybus not my father?
MESSENGER: No more than I...

The messenger's words are causing Oedipus to pass from terror to exalted confidence and hope, and Jocasta to pass from hope and confidence to terror, for she alone understands their true import. She knows that if Oedipus was not the son of Polybus, it raises the dreadful specter that he was the son of King Laius, her former husband. The messenger eagerly goes on to supply details of his birth, which to Oedipus are triumphantly reassuring, but which confirm Jocasta's worst fears beyond a shadow of a doubt. She listens most of the time in silent horror, then screams at Oedipus to stop before it is too late, rushes out, and hangs herself.

Insane Trio

In the central sequence of *King Lear*, there occurs an extraordinary confluence of madness—real, feigned, and "touched." The interaction of Lear, Edgar, and the Fool has a harrowing dramatic force and adds a weird new dimension to the tragedy.

EDGAR: Fraterretto calls me, and tells me Nero is an angler in the lake of darkness. Pray, innocent, and beware the foul fiend.

FOOL: Prithee, nuncle, tell me whether a madman be a gentleman or a yeoman.

LEAR: A king, a king!

The Spoken Word

Dramatic dialogue is not tape-recorded speech, nor is it mere conversation. It must sound natural, but it should not be an exact reproduction of talk. It is real speech, selected, shaped, and edited for dramatic purposes. It must convey the illusion of real speech.

Switch on a tape recorder behind the bar in a pub and you get hours of actual talk; but it is not talk that will be effective dramatically. Rhys Adrian, the radio and television playwright, once wrote a hilarious take-off on banal, repetitious pub conversation in a television play called *Thrills Galore*. Indirectly, it was also a burlesque of bad plays from the Slice of Life school.

Congreve believed that you could seat the two wittiest men on earth at a table with a bottle of wine and let them talk, but, as a scene in a play, it would be "coldly received by the Town."

Characterizing Speech

How is dialogue made to characterize the speaker? The characters of radio and television series are often instantly recognizable by their catch phrases. But all dramatists use them. Tesman's fussy "Hedda, fancy that!," or "Hedda, did you hear that?"; Mrs. Malaprop's verbal inaccuracies in Sheridan's *The Rivals*; Bloom's hesitating speech in Joyce's *Ulysses*—"You see," "as it happens," "as a matter of fact," "Ah yes, that's quite true"; Marmeladov's use of "Honored sir" in *Crime and Punishment*; the waiter in *You Never Can Tell*.

Hamlet's twofold or threefold iterations: "...heartily; yes, faith, heartily"; "Words, words, words"; "Very like, very like"; "Come, come, deal justly with me: come, come; nay, speak"; "except my life, except my life, except my life...."

Iago's incessant use of the first person singular:

" I am glad of this: for now I shall have reason
To show the love and duty that I bear you
With franker spirit. Therefore, as I am bound,
Receive it from me. I speak not yet of proof..."

IAGO: I see this hath a little dashed your spirits.
OTHELLO: Not a jot, not a jot.
IAGO: In faith, I fear it has.
            I hope you will consider what is spoke
            Comes from my love. But I do see you're moved.
            I am to pray you...

"My lord, for aught I know..."; "I am sorry to hear this."; "I protest I have dealt most directly in thy affair."; "I do love Cassio well...."

Who is this "I"? Only the image Iago wishes a person to see. There is no "I," only a multiplicity of false identities.

Rosalind's impetuous, imperative questions:
"Alas the day, what shall I do with my doublet and hose? What did he when thou sawest him? What said he? How looked he? Wherein went he? What makes he here? Did he ask for me? Where remains he? How parted he with thee, and when shalt thou see him again? Answer me in one word." (Act III, Scene 2)

Her trick of starting sentences with a negative or affirmative:
"Nay, you were better speak first." "No, faith, die by attorney." "No, no, Orlando..." "Ay, and twenty such." "Yes, faith, will I." "Ay, go your ways." "Nay, you might..." "Ay, but when?"

Her rapid inventories:
"...your hose should be ungartered, your bonnet unbanded, your sleeve unbuttoned, your shoe untied..."

"Tis not your inky brows, your black silk hair,
Your bugle eyeballs, nor your cheek of cream..."

Falstaff's oaths and exclamations: "By my troth" (he has no truth). "By the Lord" (he is godless). "I am a villain else" "I am a rogue if..." "I'll be damned." (He is right on all counts here.) "A plague of all cowards I say" (himself included). But no one should be too hard on Falstaff.

Other Patterns

Slang helps to fix a character's age group or class: three different generations are defined by "ripping," "super," and "groovy."

Dominant characters will usually talk in imperatives: "Do this," "Don't do that," "Tell me," "Nonsense, I insist."

A stilted, artificial language is dramatically feasible only for characters who are themselves stilted, pompous, or genteel.

Characters with grasshopper minds will fly off at a tangent in their speech, jump from subject to subject, talk in non sequiturs.

Obsessions

A character's obsessions are reflected in his most frequently used words. The Marquis de Norpois, Proust's career diplomat, is a success snob, a meritocrat. From his lips fall phrases like "success of the right sort," "a very fine position indeed," "a most authoritative source," "success has crowned his efforts," "he has won himself considerable distinction."

In Harold Pinter's *No Man's Land*, the lonely, friendless *littérateur* Spooner habitually refers to the most casual acquaintance as "a friend" of his. Briggs and Foster savagely mock him, calling him "Mr. Friend."

Dickens

Dickens is a fine model. His is a world of richly individualized people, uniquely characterized by their speech. When Sam Weller, his father, Mrs. Gamp, or Mr. Jingle open their mouths, it is they and only they who could possibly be talking.

MR. JINGLE: This way—this way—capital fun—lots of beer—hogsheads; rounds of beef—bullocks; mustard—cart loads; glorious day—down with you—make yourself at home—glad to see you—very.

SAM WELLER: Wot are you a roarin' at?... Makin' yourself so precious hot that you looks like a aggrawated glassblower. Wot's the matter?

MRS. GAMP: I takes new bread, my dear, with jest a little pat of fresh butter, and a mossel of cheese. In case there should be such a thing as a cowcumber in the 'ouse, will you be so kind as bring it, for I'm rather partial to 'em, and they does a world of good in a sick room.

Shaw cheerfully admitted he lifted some of his characters from Dickens.

Mimicry of speech patterns, "an ear," is again something that is an inborn talent. But the trick of "good, bad English"—well-structured, but ungrammatical language; sentences without verbs; half-phrased thoughts, and so on—can be learned to some extent.

Living Talk

Spoken dialogue should not be too "literary." Elegant, finely-wrought periodic sentences or long, beautiful, static descriptions of nature suit an essay or novel but are fatal in drama. Unless the dialogue sounds like real live talk that the actor can speak without stumbling, it fails.

The highest flights of the human imagination are to be found in dramatic poetry. But it is still vocal. It is written down for an actor to deliver to an audience, not to be savored only in the library. It is great poetry, but it is also great music, great song. Shaw extolled Shakespeare's word music, and his own speeches can be splendidly operatic. Even Shakespeare's grave reflections on human life become a kind of philosophy set to music.

Prose Poetry

Very naturalistic dialogue in no way precludes poetry. Mistress Quickly's description of Falstaff's death: "...I knew there was but one way; for his nose was as sharp as a pen, and 'a babbled of green fields..." Mrs. Tancred and Juno's prayer for their dead sons in *Juno and the Paycock*: "...Sacred Heart o' Jesus, take away our hearts o' stone, and give us hearts o' flesh! Take away this murdherin' hate, an' give us Thine own eternal love!" Charley's valediction over the grave of Willy Loman, ending: "A salesman is got to dream, boy. It comes with the territory."

Idiom

Idiomatic speech or dialect is important in characterizing a speaker; but it can be over-emphasized. Cockney speech where every sentence has a "Gor blimey" or "bleedin'" or "strike me pink" is self-defeating. Apart from its absurdity and lack of truth-to-life, it is indigestible. Real cockney speech can be a parody of itself, but it is the rhythm and sentence structure, as well as the actual words, that count. A skilled dramatist is very selective in the use of idiom or dialect. In the case of cockney, for example, the speech of Mr. Doolittle in *Pygmalion* is worth studying; or, more up-to-date, the characters in Pinter's *The Homecoming* or *The Caretaker*; or Edward Bond's *Saved*; or Howard Brenton's *Weapons of Happiness*.

Speech Tempo

There is much that can be achieved by the length and structure of speeches. Different structures within speeches will affect the tempo. An involved structure, with long units and emphasis on vowel sounds, will slow down the pace and convey a solemn and deliberate manner of speech.

OTHELLO: Most potent, grave and reverend signiors,
My very noble and approved good masters,
That I have ta'en away this old man's daughter,
It is most true... (Act I, Scene 3)

A speech broken up into short sentences or small units will give an impression of speed or urgency, as in Rosalind's delivery. The words tumble and cascade from her.

Speech tempo is an index of character. An instinctive ear for speech is again essential in the writing.

The tempo of a scene is governed by the dramatic situation. Changes of tempo should not be artificially imposed simply in order to achieve contrast or variety.

Dialogue Surprise

Dialogue, brilliant comic dialogue in particular, can be rich in surprise. Verbal acrobatics will keep an audience constantly on their toes. The unexpected phrase, the startling *mot juste*, a bizarre play on words, punctured clichés, sudden illogicalities, paradox, non sequiturs... They require mental double-takes by the dozen. Oscar Wilde, Joe Orton, Ionesco, Pinter, and Stoppard are masters here.

Examples

LADY BRACKNELL: ...Is this Miss Prism a female of repellent aspect, remotely connected with education?

CANON CHASUBLE: (*somewhat indignantly*): She is the most cultivated of ladies, and the very picture of respectability.

LADY BRACKNELL: It is obviously the same person. May I ask what position she holds in your household?

CANON CHASUBLE: (*severely*): I am a celibate, madam.
The Importance of Being Earnest

EDWARD: ...(*with a laugh*): You must excuse my chatting away like this. We have few visitors this time of the year. All our friends summer abroad. I'm a home bird myself. Wouldn't mind taking a trip to Asia Minor, mind you, or to certain lower regions of the Congo, but Europe? Out of the question. Much too noisy. I'm sure you agree. Now look, what will you have to drink? A glass of ale? Curaçao Fockink Orange? Ginger beer? Tia Maria? A Wachenheimer Fuchsmantel Reisling Beeren Auslese? Gin and it?...
Pinter: *A Slight Ache*

Such effects must always be in character and advance the action; otherwise they remain like unstrung gems, more suited to an anthology or book of aphorisms than a play. Wilde's brilliant epigrams in

A Woman of No Importance, for example, are often superfluous and intrusive. In the above excerpts, however, Edward is distinctly unnerved by the silent presence of the old matchseller; and the unveiling of Miss Prism's past is the vital turning-point of the plot.

Concrete Description

With obvious exceptions, such as Shavian dialectic, the concrete is preferable to the abstract in dramatic dialogue. The discussion of a relationship, particularly a love relationship, in abstract terms can become very tedious. It is more effective to illustrate it in concrete terms by a striking anecdote or memory.

Hilde Wangel does not tell Solness she fell in love with him ten years before. She describes in sharp detail the events of that day when he climbed the church tower. Alison in *Look Back in Anger* remembers in detail her first meeting with Jimmy Porter at a party.

Cassius argues fiercely (Act I, Scene 2) that Caesar is only a weak mortal by telling two vivid anecdotes: how Cassius had to save him from drowning in the Tiber after he boasted of his swimming prowess; and how Caesar shook with his fever in Spain and cried out like "a sick girl."

Anecdotes will form dramatic narratives in themselves, full of action and suspense. Greek drama is rich in narrative set-pieces. Among modern dramatists, Tennessee Williams is a master; for example, Blanche's story of her young husband's suicide in *A Streetcar Named Desire*; or the description of the death of the sea turtles in *Suddenly Last Summer*, which prepares for the play's climactic revelation.

These descriptions and narrative passages are often lengthy, however, and, like all big speeches, create traps for the unwary.

Long Speeches

Long speeches are the glory of dramatic literature, but they are dangerous to try to emulate. The more splendid the rhetoric, the greater the perils. Long speeches are unfortunately characteristic of inexperienced playwrights.

Big speeches in Greek tragedy, Shakespeare, or Racine have drama within them and behind them. They are generally drawn out forcibly by a situation highly charged with tension, where much depends on what is being said. A man may be risking his life by speaking his mind at such length and with such feeling.

News, which characters in the play have been starved of, can often be imparted in lengthy despatches, as in *The Persians* of Aeschylus.

Exposition of a mysterious and horrifying event, long concealed, can finally be delivered at great length with all the steps leading up to it, because the audience is by now burning to know; as in Tennessee Williams's *Suddenly Last Summer.* The tension is heightened even more by Catharine's refusal to remember exactly how her cousin Sebastian died. Her resistance has to be broken down by the truth drug and the doctor's relentless pressure.

Long pent-up emotion can be unleashed in a big speech, as in Henry IV's death-bed tirade against Prince Hal, when he thinks he has snatched the crown prematurely.

All Words Essential

Long speeches in the hands of a master dramatist are never "mere talk." Certainly not in Shaw, where the opposition of strong ideas within a suspense framework infuses them with drama. Every word of the Inquisitor's enormous speech in *Saint Joan* is essential. It wins what many would think impossible—a sympathy for Joan's prosecutors. This is a dramatic necessity. (See page 70.)

Long speeches are rarely without breaks, however. There are normally small interruptions—a hearer will want something confirmed, clarified, or emphasized—to make the speech more easily digestible.

Self-Confrontation

A long soliloquy or monologue in a play is still drama—generally the drama of self-confrontation. In Hamlet's case they show a man torn apart. The "rogue and peasant slave" soliloquy is a particularly fierce internal dialogue.

It is the same with the long speeches in O'Neill's *The Emperor Jones.* There is only one character in Beckett's *Krapp's Last Tape,* but he confronts his younger self through the tape recorder.

The best advice for a new writer tempted to a long speech remains: Don't. Experience is needed. Apart from anything else, ill-judged long speeches offend against economy.

Think after all what can be done with a minimum of words:

> . . .that was in another country: and besides, the wench is dead.
> . . .the unfolding star calls up the shepherd.
> Oh God! put back Thy universe and give me yesterday!
> . . .let determined things to destiny
> Hold unbewailed their way.
> . . .an ocean of salt tears could not melt the resolution of the statutes.
> . . .Good-night, sweet prince,
> And flights of angels sing thee to thy rest!

(Marlowe's *The Jew of Malta*; *Measure for Measure*; Henry Arthur Jones' *The Silver King*; *Antony and Cleopatra*; *The Crucible*; *Hamlet*.)

Economy

Dramatic dialogue should observe that strict economy so important in all areas of drama. However good a piece of dialogue may be—illuminating, entertaining, wise—if it clogs the action, it will damage the play as a whole and should come out. Splendid scenes that might appear irrelevant in successful plays will be found, on closer examination, to have an important role in the action—perhaps providing a breathing space between two hectic periods of activity.

Jaques' "All the world's a stage" in *As You Like It* neatly fills in the time while Orlando goes to fetch Adam. Despite its apparent gratuitousness, the early part of the graveyard scene effects the slow reintroduction of Hamlet after a long absence; it provides light relief; and its imagery of death and the chimeras of glory and power enrich the meaning of the play and foreshadow the tragic end. The suspense is as strong as ever. Hamlet is walking back into danger. The King is still very much alive.

Unnecessary stages in a story should be cut out. So it is with dialogue. If it is required that the main character travels from Edinburgh to London on a train, and yet it is not in the least germane to the action that he stops at every station on the way down, it will only irritate an audience and make them restless if they see him do this. Similarly, if all the irrelevant intermediate stages of a relationship are laboriously detailed in the train of a play's dialogue, the audience will become restless. They will know the play is "not getting anywhere."

Woyzeck

Büchner's *Woyzeck* is a model of dramatic concision, deserving careful study. It charts completely the life journey to catastrophe of a simple-minded, socially oppressed soldier who murders his unfaithful mistress. Its terse scenes deal only with essential dramatic points. The play says more in its twenty-five or so pages than many surviving works five times its length. As already emphasized, it has had a seminal influence on twentieth-century drama.

Leaping

At the other extreme, of course, a play can reach its climactic points much too fast and leave an audience blinking, and unconvinced. So there is an inevitable caveat to the virtue of economy. The development and growth of an action can be destroyed by crass leaps and bounds. In a few lines a man can pass from irritation to anger to murder. This may be tolerable in a black farce but nowhere else.

An audience is just as fascinated by the growth of a passion by slow gradations as it is by the depiction of that passion in full flood. If a playwright reaches conclusions too abruptly he not only blasts away plausibility, he misses many opportunities for suspense; he triggers off his explosion much too early. See what Shakespeare achieved by delaying Hamlet's revenge for four acts.

WORDS AND
SILENCE

11

Anyone who goes to a play listens to words: words carefully selected, arranged, and repeated, which create images, associative thoughts and emotions; words by which the playwright skillfully guides his audience from one state of mind or feeling to the next, wherever, in fact, he determines their collective emotion will be.

Imagery

The realm of imagery and word-association is too extensive to consider in detail. In a great play its subliminal impact on the collective emotion of an audience is immeasurable. For example, in *King Lear*, the repetition of the word and idea of "nothing," the images of pain, and the emphasis on sight and blindness running through the whole play. The bestiary, particularly the words of Poor Tom (for instance, "hog in sloth, fox in stealth, wolf in greediness, dog in madness, lion in prey") conveying with deadly insistence the idea of man in his cruelty and barbarism reeling back into the beast.

The images of darkness, night, and blood in *Macbeth*; the repetition of the words "day," "night," "yesterday," "tomorrow," and of course "time" in *Waiting for Godot*; the immense stature of Antony and Cleopatra is imagined as part of "the wide arch of the ranged Empire" they dominate: "I will piece Her opulent Throne with Kingdoms"; "His legs bestrid the Ocean; his reared arm Crested the world..."

It has rightly been said that the verbal imagery of a great play can create a kind of meta-language behind the logical language of plotting and characterization. Again, the message for new authors is: Stay clear. Acres of pretentious writing will otherwise result.

The Unspoken

Dramatic dialogue is not however confined to the spoken word. What is not said is just as important as what is, often more so. The loaded pause, the action going on within the silence, has considerable dramatic force.

Many dramatic dialogues come down to a struggle for dominance, in which silence can be used as a sword or a shield. A pause in a dialogue by Harold Pinter can be full of emotional violence. But although Pinter is a brilliant exponent of it, he did not invent the highly charged pause. It has always been part of the tension of dramatic dialogue, and it can have many resonances.

Skillful writing and acting will enable an audience practically to see thoughts, especially on television. They become almost tangible. You can watch, say, a complete mental revolution; a growing toward, a falling away; someone going far away in space or time and then returning—all between the lines. Once again this constitutes Action.

Edith Sitwell has a fine perception about the pauses that occur during the frenzied whispers between Macbeth and his Lady immediately after the murder of Duncan. For example, when Macbeth looks at his hands: "The four beats falling upon the silence before he speaks ('This is a sorry sight') seem like the sound of blood dropping, slowly, from those hands." And another, just before Macbeth demands who lies in the second chamber, when his whole inward state changes at the realization he is now a murderer, she calls: "a gap in time, like the immense gap between the Ice Age and the Stone Age, when, as Science tells us, the previously existing inhabitants of the earth were almost wholly destroyed and a different class of inhabitants created."

Radio Drama

Silence is particularly effective in radio drama. Much of the panic impact of Orson Welles's sensational *War of the Worlds* production, which led tens of thousands of Americans to believe that New York had been destroyed by invading Martians, stemmed from this. The sudden cuts, sounds fading away, the lone voice on the airwaves trying to make contact with the city: "Isn't there anyone on the air...? Isn't there...anyone?...anyone?" The answer that comes back is Nothing. It is far worse than a scream of terror.

Ingmar Bergman's film *The Seventh Seal* was originally written by him as a radio play in which Death, which is personified in the film as a man we see and hear, was represented by total silence. By all accounts its impact was more frighteningly effective on radio than in the film.

In what is arguably the finest radio play ever written—Beckett's *All That Fall*—the pauses have a searing impact. What actually happened in that train compartment? The blind old Mr. Rooney, so prone to irrational fits of rage, enters the danger zone. "My mind? Are you sure? (*Pause. Incredulous.*) My mind?... (*Pause*)." And within the pauses, the listener eerily detects filaments of insanity drifting among his thoughts.

The Sub-Text

Chekhov's characters often don't talk at all about the things that most concern them. In the famous short scene at the end of *The Cherry Orchard*, Lopakhin and Varya are left alone together in order that he can propose to her. He fails to. They talk about anything but that—packing, going away, the coldness of the weather—and heartbreak occurs beneath the surface of this apparently trivial talk. Coward used much the same method in the first act of *Private Lives*, where there is a dichotomy between what characters say and what they want. The brittle chat between Elyot and Amanda ("Very big, China") is amusing, but at the same time they are desperately trying to keep their true feelings, which are threatening to become overwhelming, in check.

Woody Allen cleverly combined words and thoughts in one scene in his film *Annie Hall*. He and Diane Keaton chat uneasily while subtitles, telling us their real thoughts about each other, are flashed on the screen. In Peter Nichols' *Passion Play* the characters' alter egos come on stage with them and speak their thoughts.

Langrishe, Go Down _____

In Harold Pinter's screenplay of Aidan Higgins's novel *Langrishe, Go Down*, which was directed as a BBC Television film by David Jones, the following scene takes place on a stair landing between two sisters, Imogen and Helen. Helen has just stolen Imogen's love letters.

(HELEN *is ascending the stairs.* IMOGEN *comes into shot on the landing.*)

IMOGEN: Oh Helen...

(HELEN *stops*)

HELEN: Yes? What is it?

IMOGEN: Could I have a word with you?

HELEN: Surely.

(HELEN *walks up toward her.*)
Two shot. Landing.

HELEN: What is it?
(*Pause*)

IMOGEN: I was just wondering...why you...I mean...if you...
(*Pause*)

HELEN: If I what?
(*Pause*)

IMOGEN: Well, I just wondered...

HELEN: You wondered what?
(*Pause*)

IMOGEN: Have you been in my room?
(*Pause*)

HELEN: For what purpose?
(*Pause*)

IMOGEN: Well, it's of no importance, really. It's really of little importance.
(*Pause*)
So.

(IMOGEN *turns out of shot.* HELEN *turns, in opposite direction.*)

Imogen confronts Helen and attempts to challenge her. Helen dares her to continue. Imogen is intimidated and fails to go through with it. It is what is not said that charges the scene with dramatic tension. (In the film Judi Dench played Imogen; Annette Crosbie, with icy composure, played Helen.)

Here the pauses of the author were gauged with a fine precision. It should be mentioned, however, that they can be exaggerated, held longer than necessary, given an unwarranted "significance." Harold Pinter himself is well aware of this. When he was directing his own play *The Hothouse* for BBC Television, he gave a talk to the cast. Referring to one particular speech, he instructed the actor to "shorten the spaces between the sentences: I don't want this to become a *Pinter-pausey* play."

Hemingway

Among novelists, Hemingway was a master of tip-of-the-iceberg dialogue. Not only did it all happen beneath what was actually spoken, but the memory of a Hemingway novel or story can include vivid scenes that, on return to the text, cannot be found. They were fed into the reader's imagination by implication only. Ben Hecht, working as a screenwriter on *A Farewell to Arms*, said, "That S.O.B. writes in WATER!"

Ibsen's *Rosmersholm*

What really happens below the surface in *Rosmersholm* is awesome. The dense, oblique colloquies batten down over the tremendous pressure of moral murder, incest, and searing guilt. The actual words that are uttered are extracted with great difficulty from the tensions of the situation.

The schoolmaster, Kroll, whose sister Beata has been driven to suicide by Rebecca West, relentlessly interrogates her about her paternity.

KROLL: ...my calculation may be correct all the same. Because Dr. West paid your district a brief visit the year before he became employed there.

REBECCA: (*cries*): That's a lie!

KROLL: Is it?

REBECCA: Yes. My mother never mentioned that.

KROLL:	Didn't she?
REBECCA:	No. Never. Nor Dr. West. Not a word.
KROLL:	Might that not have been because they both had reason to forget a year? Just as you have done, Miss West. Perhaps it's a family trait.
REBECCA:	(*walks around, twisting and untwisting her hands*): It isn't possible. It's only something you're trying to make me imagine. It can't be true. It can't! Not possibly—!
KROLL:	(*gets up*): But my dear—why in heaven's name are you taking it so to heart? You quite frighten me. What am I to imagine—?
REBECCA:	Nothing. You are to imagine nothing.
KROLL:	Then you really must explain to me why this fact—this possibility, if you like—so alarms you?
REBECCA:	(*composes herself*): It's quite simple, Dr. Kroll. I just don't want people to think of me as illegitimate.
KROLL:	I see. Well, let's settle for that explanation—for the moment.

The true explanation is hidden beneath the suggestion that Dr. West was Rebecca's real as well as adoptive father. The shocking recognition of her probable incest—which she almost betrays—would compound her guilt intolerably and impel her toward self-destruction. This powerful motive operates as a deep unspoken force in the drama.

Note the question-and-answer method here, and in the previous example from *Oedipus Rex*. Kroll and Oedipus strive to get at the truth in these scenes and meet resistance. Detective-story techniques can apply to the greatest classics as well as the most ephemeral Shaftesbury Avenue or Broadway thriller.

Fatal Imitations

Novice playwrights should steer clear of the sub-text. If they grapple with it, they are likely to achieve a surface banality and no underlying action. This happens with so many first plays that are derivative of the work of Harold Pinter, for example. Their authors fail to discern the real action within the dialogue they try to imitate.

In general, Pinter, Beckett, and Chekhov should be approached warily by playwrights during their apprenticeship. They would do better to concentrate on Barrie, Maugham, Rattigan, and Ibsen plays such as *An Enemy of the People*, *Hedda Gabler*, and *The Wild Duck*.

THE SCENARIO

12

An aspiring young playwright consulted Ibsen about a play he was thinking of writing. "Where is your scenario?" Ibsen asked. When the young man derided the idea of scenarios, Ibsen showed him the door. He always wrote detailed scenarios himself, and some are preserved, as are the first drafts of his plays, in *From Ibsen's Workshop*, edited by Archer.

A scenario lays bare the skeleton of the whole play. The curve of the action is there, all the main elements of suspense, preparation and complication, goals, obstacles, climax, and resolution.

A good dramatic scenario is often lengthy. It must be distinguished from a mere outline or synopsis.

It is sometimes argued, as the young man probably did to Ibsen, that play writing is unplanned—the Muse strikes, and the play flows effortlessly onto the page. More understandably, but still wrongly, it is said that the scenario is a strait-jacket, that it is too rigid a framework and does not allow for new ideas or characters taking on a life of their own.

Flexibility and Proportion _____

But a good scenario is not inflexible: it is loose-jointed; it leaves avenues open. Even if the writing of the dialogue has begun and new ideas then press in with a force that cannot be ignored, this still does not constitute an argument against scenarios. In this event, it is better to dismantle the whole play and write a new scenario incorporating the new ideas. In the long run it will save time.

If the playwright uses scenarios imaginatively, the whole framework of the play, properly shaped and proportioned, will be there before he gets down to the detail of the dialogue.

It requires patience to write scenarios, as well as restraint. The impulse to rush into dialogue is often very hard to resist. But what is the use of that colorful scene, that smart new character incident, if it fatally impedes the action or throws the entire play off balance? Proportioning the play, seeing it whole: this is the value of the scenario. Without it, time can be wasted, enthusiasm drain away, and discouragement set in.

False Resolutions _____

A familiar result of unplanned play writing, in the case of a three-act play, is a couple of good acts and a dud last act. The author often cannot understand why the third act will not come right. But it is the basic concept of the play as a whole that is at fault, and the only hope is to dismantle it altogether. This means two acts have been wasted, and painfully so, because they did come to life and have now to be abandoned. A common cause is that the resolution does not grow naturally out of the action. It has to be grafted on and so betrays the play's shaky foundations.

With a good scenario as a guide the playwright has an early warning system. It will indicate, for example, what has to be sign-posted, when, and how; what has to be held back, and the right moment for its entry; and it will enable the writer to keep the play's crisis and resolution constantly in mind, and so give a unity and shape to the whole.

The major crisis of a play is like a great waterfall or vortex, whose powerful undertow draws all toward it at a faster and faster rate. We are conscious of it as we watch the play. The playwright should be even more conscious of it as he writes it. A scenario will keep his destination constantly in mind.

Example: *A Dolls' House* _____

The most detailed scenario left by Ibsen was for *A Doll's House*. Here is the conclusion of the second act (Krogstad's letter to Nora's husband will shatter their marriage):

> ...Scene between Krogstad and Nora—She entreats and implores him for the sake of her little children; in vain. Krogstad goes out. The letter is seen to fall from outside into the (locked) letter-box.—Mrs. Linde re-enters after a short pause. Scene between her and Nora. Half confession. Mrs. Linde goes out.—Nora alone.—Stenborg (Ibsen's original name for Nora's husband) enters. Scene between him and Nora. He wants to empty the letter-box. Entreaties, jests, half playful persuasion. He promises to let business wait till after New Year's Day; but at 12 o'clock midnight—! Exit. Nora alone. Nora (looking at the clock): It is five o'clock. Five:—seven hours till midnight. Twenty-four hours till the next midnight. Twenty-four and seven—thirty-one. Thirty-one hours to live.—

Note how the scenario charts the build-up of suspense.

The first draft of the play, which Ibsen wrote from the scenario, changed considerably in the revision and rewriting, so much so that the first draft became a kind of super-scenario. Many of the elements that make *A Doll's House* so truthful and penetrating developed in this later rewriting. The play's most famous line "Millions of women have done so" was added as an after-thought.

Every writer must find his own way of working. But Ibsen's method is a formidable one. Would-be playwrights disregard it at their peril.

VISION AND
PERFORMANCE I

13

However glorious its language, a play is written to be seen and heard. The great nineteenth-century English poets attempted to write plays and failed, because they thought that language alone was enough. They ignored actors, audience, and visual effects altogether, let alone the techniques for holding the audience's attention. (Shakespeare, a working man of the theater, knew better.)

As a critic, Coleridge saw that "the power of poetry is, by a single word perhaps, to instill that energy into the mind which compels the imagination to produce the picture." His statement is very appropriate for the bare Elizabethan stage, and also for a medium he never knew. In radio drama, a few carefully selected words can bring a whole landscape into the mind of the listener, as surely as the sketch pad of a great Impressionist painter brings a landscape before his eyes.

Theater Images

But an audience thinks with its eyes too. Spectacle is a very important element in theater, reaching its apotheosis probably in the music dramas of Wagner. Visual metaphors are very potent. Beckett's for example: two tramps standing by a tree on an empty country road (*Waiting for Godot*); a woman sinking slowly into a mound of earth under a fierce sun (*Happy Days*); a mouth babbling away in a small spotlight surrounded by stage blackness (*Not I*).

Hamlet looking at Yorick's skull, Willy Loman with his cases of samples, Mother Courage pulling her wagon, Joan with her sword and armor, Prospero and his staff... Long stage tradition has created these images that have as much impact as the spoken word. Great plays are emphatically not meant for the study: they are meant for the stage.

Poetry on Film

There is a poetry of cinema and television. Cocteau's *Orphée* or Bergman's *Wild Strawberries*, with their haunting dream imagery, cannot be discussed in any other terms.

Cocteau has several superb images in *Orphée*: the black motorcycle outriders of death, a perfect contemporary parallel for angels of death; the mirror that turns to water as Orpheus passes through it—another image of death; and his walk through the ruined zone of winds that vividly realizes his journey to the underworld.

Wild Strawberries starts with a nightmare in which the eminent old physician, who is the central character of the film, approaches a coffin that has fallen from a hearse in a blazing white street in horrible circumstances and broken open. A hand reaches out, grabs his arm, and pulls him in toward the coffin. He sees that the man inside the coffin is—himself. The sequence underscores the film's theme that throughout his life he has destroyed his own capacity for human feeling.

2001

In Stanley Kubrick's film *2001: A Space Odyssey*, great imagery is used to convey the irony of progress when a primitive ape-man discovers his first tool—a bone—at the dawn of history. Finding he can also use it as a weapon to kill animals and fellow creatures, he throws it triumphantly into the air in slow motion. As it begins slowly to fall, the bone changes, by a brilliant split-second associative cut, into a space satellite, probably carrying nuclear weapons, orbiting the earth at the end of the twentieth century.

Both the dark, brooding silhouette of the Malvern Hills and the bright, sunlit sweep of the Malverns, in their different ways, dominated David Rudkin's BBC Television play *Penda's Fen*, directed by Alan Clarke, and Ken Russell's film on Elgar. In the one, the hills were satanic and bloodstained; in the other they were Elysian. But the image set the whole tone and atmosphere for both works.

Strindberg

Strindberg's dream plays, with their fluidity, rapid transitions, and expressionistic imagery, anticipated the sophisticated techniques of cinema and television by sixty years. They require brilliant direction to succeed in the theater. This happened with Bergman's 1970 production of *A Dream Play*. Its startling images included the macabre degree ceremony; the coal carriers propping up civilized society; and the blind man on the shore with a child beside him waving farewell to a ship, her handkerchief drawing an invisible line through the air.

No Words

A story can be told without words. In the silent film, a succession of images is enough; even the captions that are flashed on the screen can become an intrusion after a time. The story of *Hamlet* or *Macbeth* could be made comprehensible to an audience if it were mimed.

Many sequences in theater, film, and television work perfectly well without words. The audience can safely be left to draw the right conclusions. They make the narrative connections themselves. They can see, for example, thoughts forming, plots being laid, temptation aroused, hopes dashed, without the aid of dialogue. "The vital scenes of a drama," said Moss Hart, "are played as much by the audience as by the actors on stage."

Screenwriting

The art of the screenwriter, as distinct from the playwright, is to write the pictures as well as the dialogue. In this, his skills embrace those of the novelist. The Mankiewicz and Welles screenplay for *Citizen Kane* starts with the camera moving through the great gardens of Kane's castle of Xanadu. His exotic domain is captured with phrases like "Angkor Wat, the night the last King died"..."An ironic reference to Indian temple bells."

Eisenstein, the great Russian director, virtually admitted he used *Paradise Lost* as a shooting script for his film *Alexander Nevsky*. He interpreted one of Milton's phrases—"nearer view"—as an instruction to move from long shot to medium shot.

In Close

Film and television have a grammar of their own that can tell a story with high precision and economy. Cutting away to reaction shots of other people can offer an eloquent comment on what a character has said. The rhythm and pace of a film can be controlled by quick cutting or shots held for a long time. The use of close-ups means that an actor needs to project far less on film or television. The camera shows minute changes of facial expression that tell all. The performances of Alec Guinness and Ian Richardson as spy-catcher and "mole" in the BBC Television serial of John le Carré's *Tinker Tailor Soldier Spy* were remarkable instances of this; as was that of Jeremy Irons in Granada TV's shining production of Waugh's *Brideshead Revisited*. Or Michael Bryant as Mathieu in Sartre's *Roads to Freedom*—directed for the BBC by James Cellan Jones—still the finest classic serial ever shown on British television.

This again proves that the screenwriter or television dramatist needs fewer words. A flicker of an eyelid can make three or four explanatory lines redundant.

Montage

Montage in film making is the assembly of a succession of images that, by juxtaposition and rapid cutting, creates a chain of associative ideas. Without words, it can advance the action and enrich the texture of the film.

The film audience can be made to feel fear without actually being told to feel it. Hitchcock said: "The menace should be transferred from the screen into the minds of the audience." Consider Antonioni's famous seven-minute wordless shot at the end of *The Passenger*.

Locke, played by Jack Nicholson, who has swapped identities with a mysterious gun-runner, lies in a hotel room behind the camera which is at a window looking out on a square in Algeciras. His girlfriend, who has just been talking with him, waits tensely in the square, because he has asked to be left alone. But she knows he is probably in some kind of danger. There is silence, stillness. Cars arrive. An African we know to be a government agent gets out of one and walks to the hotel. Behind the camera is heard the sound of a door opening, then a muffled report: it could be a traffic noise, a falling object, or a shot from a pistol. Stillness again. Locke's anxious wife arrives in a police car. The camera is now moving slowly out into the square; it turns through 180 degrees, then closes in on the window from the outside as the urgent group makes for the hotel. Finally we see Locke dead, facing the wall, the two women and the police with him. He probably has been assassinated, though he could have died of a heart attack like the man whose place he took.

Words and Image

If a point can be made successfully without words, therefore, it achieves more economy and concentration. Paradoxically, this does not reduce the importance of words but heightens it. It makes every word vital. It is a major portion of the screenwriter or television dramatist's skill to match those vital words to the image. It is also central to the art of directing in any visual medium.

The Co-Author

The actor has been called the co-author of the play. It is a statement that would probably have appalled Wordsworth or Shelley, but every working dramatist knows its truth.

A play's text, said Baker, is a kind of shorthand for the actor to flesh out. It comes as a surprise to the inexperienced writer to read what is actually written down on the page, which created such a devastating effect when he saw it. It will often strike him as commonplace, grey writing. A passage that had the whole audience rocking with laughter, or on the edge of their seats with suspense, can look as flat as the musical score of a symphony, compared with its actual performance.

Play Reading

Good dialogue can sometimes appear unintelligible on the page to any but an experienced play reader. It is necessary to read between the lines and beneath the words, to understand tones of voice, and to visualize what is happening for its logic and sense to become clear.

A trained play reader often finds all but the greatest novels an irritation: They tell so much more than is necessary for anyone who responds quickly to what is happening in a passage of spare dramatic dialogue. Kenneth Tynan reportedly said that novels were just "padded stage directions."

Brought to Life

Most dramatic situations can be fully appreciated only when we see them acted out, whether it is a woman watching a man she is in love with exchange a meaningful look with another woman; or a man crassly letting slip a vital secret that only one other person in the group spots; or a father suspiciously watching his daughter growing too friendly with a young man he regards as an unsuitable match; or two assassins seeing a man talking to their potential victim and, as they think, warning him of their enterprise.

Reactions are seldom disclosed by the text. It is Hamlet and the King we watch during *The Murder of Gonzago*, not the Players. We mainly watch Célimène, not Arsinoé, during Arsinoé's catty speech to her about her shortcomings in *The Misanthrope*. We watch Constantine even more than Nina, when she tells of her passionate love for Trigorin in the last act of *The Seagull*, because it is a mortal blow to him. Indeed, without containing a single "poetic" phrase, a Chekhov play as a whole can constitute a poem when performed in the theater.

Vocal Range

When all the visual impact the actor is capable of making—facial expression, gesture, bodily movement—is combined with the full range of his vocal effects, the truth about joint authorship becomes apparent. The words can ring out, as Shaw said, "like a thousand trumpets," or they can be uttered with infinitely subtle shades of meaning.

An understanding of nuance is vital in dramatic writing. An audience can often be told all that it needs to know by the intonation and inflection of the voice. A simple phrase like: "Get away" can be varied by the speaker to convey totally different things. A "Yes" or "No" or "Indeed" can have many implications and resonances depending on how it is said. Edith Evans did wonders with Lady Bracknell's two words, "A handbag?" It is no accident that many dramatists have been actors themselves.

Great Actors

Brecht records that when he was working with Charles Laughton on the 1947 production of *Galileo*, he was struck by Laughton's cavalier attitude to dramatic masterpieces. He regarded them as so many "scripts" designed to go off in performance like gunpowder. Brecht's view of Laughton was admiring as well as rueful. The role of co-author is a formidable one. Great actors do seize classic plays as vehicles for themselves. If this is reprehensible, the audiences who flock to see them do not appear unduly worried. A play, moreover, is often written with a particular actor or actress in mind.

Four Examples

1. *The Map of Africa*

This passage of dialogue occurs at the end of Chekhov's *Uncle Vanya*:

MARINA:	You're not going off without any tea?
ASTROV:	I don't want any, Nanny.
MARINA:	A little vodka then?
ASTROV:	(*hesitantly*): Well, perhaps—

(MARINA *goes out*)

ASTROV:	(*After a pause*): My trace horse has gone a bit lame. I noticed it yesterday when Petrushka was taking him to water.
VOYNITSKY:	You'll have to get him reshod.
ASTROV:	I'd better call in at the blacksmith's in Rozhdestvennoye. There's nothing else for it. (*Goes up to the map of Africa and looks at it*). Down there in Africa the heat must be quite something. Terrific!
VOYNITSKY:	Very probably.
MARINA:	(*returning with a glass of vodka and a piece of bread on a tray*): Here you are.

(ASTROV *drinks the vodka*)

MARINA:	Your health, my dear. (*Bows low*). Why not have a little bread with it?
ASTROV:	No, it'll do as it is. All the best to you then. (*To* MARINA). Don't bother to see me to the door, Nanny, there's no need. (*He goes out.* SONYA *goes after him with a candle to see him off.*)

On the page, its dramatic values are in no way apparent. But in performance, set in its context, it is electric. Voynitsky (Vanya) has just humiliated himself again. He has stolen a bottle of morphia from Dr. Astrov's case with the intention of committing suicide, and has been pressured by Astrov and Sonya into giving it back. Sonya is in love with Astrov. It is unrequited, and Astrov has been asked to spare her feelings by not calling at the house again. He has just told her he will not be back for some time. The carriage is waiting, and he wants to get away; but, a seasoned drinker, he is tempted by the offer of vodka from the old nurse Marina, who knows nothing of the circumstances. Vanya, in despair, has to sit there doing his accounts, wishing Astrov would just get out of the place. Sonya wants Astrov to linger, but she too is badly hurt and knows she has little prospect of seeing him again. (Anna Calder–Marshall in a Royal Court production sat at the table in these minutes, her hand shielding her eyes, but acutely aware of his presence.) They are in

Vanya's study which, like his character, is full of odd furnishings. On the wall is a map of Africa. In the tension following Marina's exit to fetch the vodka, it forces Astrov to make a banal remark. It enables Vanya to make a dry reply. (Africa is also a faraway place—and far away is where Astrov would very much like to be at this moment, even farther than the blacksmith's at the place with the long name.) It is both a tragic and a comic scene, full of feeling, charged with cross-rhythms and tensions, which, properly played, will hold an audience spellbound. Yet on the page it is flat and uninteresting.

2. *The Barometer on the Piano*

In the last act of Coward's *Hay Fever*, the following exchange takes place:

MYRA: Where's the barometer?
RICHARD: On the piano.
MYRA: What a queer place for it to be!

Properly pointed and timed, this innocuous passage will bring the house down with laughter. Why? It is Sunday morning. All the guests are eager to sneak out of the Bliss household and get away from this ghastly weekend. Richard has just come gingerly downstairs, seen the rain, and tapped the barometer. It has fallen off the wall and broken. Very embarrassed, but not wanting to waste time, he has put it on the piano, perhaps hoping it will not be noticed. Myra, another guest, enters, and in her blasé way comments on the absence of the barometer. Richard chokes over his breakfast and says where it is. Fleshed out by fine comic acting, the sequence is extremely funny in the theater. Yet it signifies little on the page.

3. *Wingate*

In BBC Television's *Wingate Trilogy* by Don Shaw, this passage occurs in the script, after Orde Wingate has reinstated the Emperor of Ethiopia on his throne:

HAILE SELASSIE: I would like to name a town or a place after you. What place do you prefer?
WINGATE: I would prefer nothing if it's to be associated with cruelty.
HAILE SELASSIE: Colonel Wingate, what cruelty?

On screen Wingate, played by Barry Foster, is seen forcing back his anger after the Emperor's first statement. After delivering his cryptically insolent answer, he turns on his heel and walks away down the long hall of the palace. He almost reaches the door when the Emperor stops him with the words, "Colonel Wingate." Wingate turns. Another loaded pause. The Emperor's question. Wingate then elaborates on his grievance—Haile Selassie is shooting collaborators. Moments charged with tension in performance. On the page, a spare blueprint.

4. *Nicholas Nickleby*

In the Royal Shakespeare Company's production of *Nicholas Nickleby*, Kate Nickleby's mother is taken to the opera by some unsavory gentry led by Sir Mulberry Hawk. Kate is also there in an adjoining box with her party. She greets her mother with astonishment, but is shocked to find her with the louts who have been making her life a misery. They all change places, Sir Mulberry contriving to get close to Kate. He has ingratiated himself with Mrs. Nickleby for this purpose. But they must continue to pay attention to the mother, who turns a blind eye to Kate's discomfiture. The result is an entertaining gavotte, or game of musical chairs, to the accompaniment of the opera, which takes place above them on a raised platform. Not a word of dialogue is needed in the scene. The actions tell everything, and involve suspense, surprise, irony, and comic embarrassment.

VISION AND
PERFORMANCE II

Plays in Rehearsal: The Role of the Director _____

Watching many plays in performance, including audience reaction, combined whenever possible with a study of the text, is very much part of a playwright's training.

Watching plays in rehearsal, particularly his own, is an even more valuable experience for him. He will rapidly discover whether something he has written will work. If not, he and the artists can try out alternatives that will. Much rewriting can be done during rehearsals or out-of-town previews.

The Secret Play

A director working with actors in a rehearsal room will dig into the text to discover its meaning. This can be difficult and requires patience. In a good play there is so much going on at many levels. It is the job of the director and his artists to find it. More than one noted director talks of the "secret play" that can be discovered only during rehearsals.

Partnership

A good director will not dictate unless it is absolutely necessary, in which case there was probably a mistake in casting. He will not give inflections but will talk about motivations and make certain everyone, including himself, knows what is happening in the scene. If he lays down the law too early he loses a great deal, because, by leaving it open to the actors, they can surprise him with a totally different way of doing it, more effective than any instruction he may have given. It is essentially a partnership with the cast, though finally the director will have to act as umpire. If he generates the right atmosphere—humor helps a great deal—his authority is unlikely to be questioned.

Experimentation

A director and actors will experiment, trying a scene first one way, then another. The same scene can indeed be played in very different ways. It has been known for Osric to get the better of Hamlet and do it convincingly. Peter Brook's great production of *King Lear* brought home to audiences that Goneril and Regan had a valid case against their father, deserving of sympathy. As a Henry V who had yet to attain full manhood, Alan Howard successfully delivered "Once more unto the breach, dear friends" as though he were not entirely confident it was the best course of action.

There are no definitive interpretations, though it is certainly true that one performance can overshadow others for a generation: Gielgud's Hamlet, Olivier's Richard III. Gielgud's powerful performance as Cassius in the film of *Julius Caesar* gave a striking new view of the play. Here, indeed, was the driver of the action.

Choice of Words

Directing is a subtle process of suggestion, needing a careful choice of words—the right adjective, the right adverb. . . . The kind of things that might be heard during rehearsals are "She says that to duck the emotional climate." "Irony." "Very grand—she's already trying on the Lady Mayoress's chain." "That throws him." "She's beginning to have second thoughts here." "His mind's on what's just happened in the previous scene." "Defeated." "Mocking." "She's heard it all before." "Contempt." "If he sounds off there, it leaves him nowhere to go." "Think less about the *how*, more about the *what*." "Enjoy that line more."

When the distraught Constantine lays the dead seagull at Nina's feet in Chekhov's *The Seagull*, she says, "What does that signify?" If the director is playing up the comedy, he might say to the actress: "Her tone is 'You'll be giving me your ear next.'"

A director illuminates the text in the same way as a novelist. Tolstoy writes a line for Anna Karenina and then comments on it: "'That only shows you have no heart,' she said. But her eyes said that she knew he had a heart, and that was why she was afraid of him." See this translated into dramatic terms. The playwright writes Anna's line, the director comments that it is completely at variance with what she really thinks and feels, then leaves it to the actress to realize it. He may correct her later if she signals it insufficiently or too strongly.

Director and actors might also talk about the history of the characters, or validly construct one from hints dropped by the playwright.

Spontaneity

The director aims for freshness and spontaneity. The cast knows the whole play, and each actor knows what line is coming up; but they wouldn't in life, and the audience does not know. The play should be performed as though the events are happening for the very first time.

Movement

The director and cast will need to choreograph the play's action. This will not be confined to practical problems such as centralizing the most important character or the focal point of the action, highlighting a significant entrance, or getting people off the stage unobtrusively.

The play's vital energy often finds expression in physical movement. But it must spring naturally from the situation and be in character. Yes, he is shy, he would go and look at the bookcase. No, that move is false; stand still. Yes, she is seething with anger at that point; it would be in character for her to pace about the stage.

The Maltese Falcon

When Humphrey Bogart as Sam Spade casually mentions to Mary Astor that he has seen Joel Cairo, she tries to cover her agitation by rising from her seat and poking the fire. He is amused by the movement. "You're good. You're very good," he comments ironically. They are both acting very much in character.

Knowing the problems that are likely to occur, the playwright can anticipate them. Visualizing the performance as he writes, he can devise movements and build them into the dialogue and the emotional action. Shaw used chess pieces to work out the movements of his characters.

The Shrew

Shakespeare, who hardly ever gives specific stage directions, directs movement through the dialogue alone by rhythm, pace, and facts. "Why does the world report that Kate doth limp?" Petruchio taunts Katharine in *The Taming of the Shrew*; "O, let me see thee walk." Kate has to move to make sense of the dialogue. But Shakespeare leaves it to the artists to work out the details. Note the movement implicit in the passage from *Antony and Cleopatra* quoted on page 92.

Stillness

Movement and stillness, if truthful, are equally dramatic. Tennessee Williams gains much dramatic mileage from Brick's restricted movement in *Cat on a Hot Tin Roof*, where he is forced to hobble about on a crutch. Sheridan Whiteside's immobility in *The Man Who Came to Dinner* is the basic situation of the play. Brian Clark in his play *Who's Life Is It Anyway?* built his dramatic situation on the central character's paralysis from the neck down.

Pre-Direction

It is no bad thing for the author as he writes his play to be directing it in his own mind, seeing it all the time from the viewpoint of the audience. In the case of films, many of the best screenplays are in a sense pre-directed. The script, however, should not be packed with elaborately binding stage or camera directions by the author.

The greatest dramatists can often by the way they write the

line direct the actor how to deliver it, complete even with gesture and facial expression, for example, Cleopatra's "Now I see, I see, In Fulvia's death, how mine received shall be."; or Antony's "Grates me! The sum." when told of the news from Rome; or the example from *Othello* on page 100.

Granville Barker

Essentially the director should be a catalyst, bringing the author's text to life in splendid performances. Some of the best "notes" on record are Granville Barker's to John Gielgud when the latter played King Lear at the Old Vic in 1940. For example, he locates the precise moment at which Lear goes mad:

> I believe that Poor Tom's appearance from the hovel marks it . . . The Fool's scream of terror and the wild figure suddenly appearing would be enough to send him over the border-line.
>
> . . . . Lear remains on knees at end of prayer, head buried in hands. At the sound of Edgar's "Fathom and half . . ." Lear lifts his head. Face seen through his outspread fingers (suggestion of madman looking through bars).
>
> The Fool screams and runs on. This gets Lear to his feet. He turns towards the hovel, watching intently for what will emerge.
>
> Edgar's entrance and speech. Lear immensely struck by it *cf.* Hamlet—Ghost . . . As he turns to speak, we see that he is now quite off his head.
>
> Dead silence before you say (in a voice you have not used before) "Didst thou give all to thy daughters?"
>
> I believe this may be right. Worth trying anyhow.

Brilliant perceptions combined with practical suggestions. The director has done his work well. He now leaves it to the artist to create the magic on stage.

VISION AND
PERFORMANCE III

Shakespeare's Torch-Bearers _____

My accounts of six supreme dramatic moments.

Brook's Dream

Peter Brook used the devices of the Chinese circus in his famous production of *A Midsummer Night's Dream*. At one remarkable point Oberon and Puck descended on their trapezes. The "little western flower" had been transformed into a silver plate which Puck spun on a metal wand with a high-pitched humming sound, and then passed to Oberon who caught it spinning on his wand. As the trapezes leveled out, the humming stopped, and Alan Howard as Oberon spoke the lines: "I know a bank where the wild thyme blows..."

The visual impact of the dazzling white set, the rich mauve and yellow costumes, the graceful descent of the trapezes, the skill, timing, and suspense—would the plate fall?—the haunting sound, then, in the sudden silence, Howard's voice, soft and low yet with an edge of steel, speaking the superb poetry, created a true moment of magic in the theater.

Judi Dench as Hermione

Trevor Nunn's production of *The Winter's Tale* for the Royal Shakespeare Company forcibly elucidated King Leontes' sudden access of jealousy, when he sees his Queen talking vivaciously with his best friend Polixenes (Act I, Scene 2). By alternating normal stage lighting with eerie blue strobe lighting, and including mimed erotic sequences to represent the King's delusions, the production showed how harmless social behavior could be misinterpreted by a jealous mind.

Central to this achievement was the performance of Judi Dench as Queen Hermione. Of all the subtle changes she effected during the scene, probably the most striking was when she had to say "He something seems unsettled" about Leontes, who had begun to show signs of instability. In the blue light she endowed the line with a sinister rhythm, a cruel taunting lilt, extending the last syllable of "unsettled," as though the Queen really were cuckolding her husband and mocking him for it. We instantly saw her through Leontes' jealous eyes. Suddenly the blue light cut out, normality returned with the warm light of the court, and she came forward to her husband with Polixenes, genuinely concerned over the fact that he was upset about something and wanting to know what it was: "Are you moved, my lord?" The alternations applied throughout the scene, by the end of which the audience totally understood Leontes' state of mind.

Judi Dench as Beatrice

Judi Dench again showed her mastery of the sudden change that can quell or reinstate a mood at will in John Barton's production for the RSC of *Much Ado About Nothing*.

Does Beatrice's "merry war" of words with Benedick conceal a real wound? She talks mischievously and laughingly about him to Don Pedro (Act II, Scene 1). Carrying the audience with her on this happy sparkling note, Miss Dench's smiling face suddenly darkened, and she froze the theater into silence with the line "Once before he won it (that is, my heart) of me with false dice." We glimpsed a whole history. She and Benedick had an affair before which ended unhappily; he had hurt her badly. This was only for an instant. Miss Dench returned just as suddenly to laughter, and the audience relaxed. But for a moment the comic mask had slipped, and we saw possible tragedy beneath.

Olivier as Shylock

In Jonathan Miller's production of *The Merchant of Venice* for the National Theatre, the trial scene was over. Shylock, played by Laurence Olivier, had left the stage, a ruined, humiliated, and dying man.

Suddenly the audience was startled by a sound off stage. Instinctively they knew the sound was human, though it hit the ears at first like a pane of glass breaking, or tin plates clattering down stone steps. It was in fact Shylock sobbing, retching up his grief in hacking jerks and spasms, as a consumptive coughs up blood. The sobbing declined into a low moaning, a keening, thinner and thinner until it died away.

It cast a horrific chill over the theater. The dialogue winding up the scene was barely registered. Olivier's dreadful cry of agony darkened the entire last act. Which is just: no one should enjoy Belmont after that. At the play's end, Shylock's daughter Jessica was left by herself on stage. The Jewish prayer for the dead was heard. She was alone in an alien Christian world.

Olivier's Richard III

Richard of Gloucester is proclaimed King by the citizens of London in a farce engineered by his cronies, the Duke of Buckingham, Catesby, and others. A charade is played out in which Richard pretends he does not want the crown, and finally accepts it with seeming great reluctance. He is in a gallery, wrapped in a hypocritical cloak of piety, and flanked by two bishops. When the ritual is complete, he knows the throne is his.

In the film, which paralleled his stage performance, Laurence Olivier, as Richard, watched the crowd disperse, then pushed the bishops away, swung down the bell rope to the ground, and waited.

The audience now witnessed a sudden transformation from the charade to the brutal realities of power. Buckingham and other henchmen ran toward him eagerly. Richard shot out his arm and pointed to the ground. He was now King, they his subjects. Compelled by the force of his will, they knelt at his feet in homage and Buckingham kissed his hand. Richard was dressed in black; his face, lifted skywards, had a ghastly pallor, and his eyes were bleak and remote; his crooked body weirdly disjointed, he trailed the robber barons like mastiffs on a leash. His tyranny was already a fact.

Overhead the bell tolled the death knell of England's freedom and the inauguration of a reign of terror.

It was an unforgettable image. There are no stage directions for it in *Richard III*. Shakespeare knew what he was doing, though. He created all the conditions for just such a magnificent stroke by a great actor. It was totally in character for Richard to act thus, and the way is thoroughly paved for it in the text.

Olivier's Othello

Laurence Olivier as Othello was a purple firestorm, and the National Theatre audience reeled under its scorching heat. The climax to the temptation scene was probably its greatest moment. As Hazlitt said of Edmund Kean, Olivier "filled every part of the stage." He delivered the speech about the Pontic sea directly outward, his eyes and hands tracking with mesmeric power its remorseless, compulsive course to the Hellespont.

> Even so my bloody thoughts with violent pace
> Shall ne'er look back, ne'er ebb to humble love,
> Till that a capable and wide revenge
> Swallow them up. Now, by yond marble heaven,
> In the due reverence of a sacred vow
> I here engage my words.

In this moment, the words were crushed, melted down, and extended. "Ne'er" became "ne-eee-er." "Marble" became a barbaric howl, almost a line on its own: "ma..aaa..arble." Most searing was Othello's inability now to get his tongue round the word "love." He stammered "l-l-l-" for an agonizing yawning gap of time, till he completed the word, then roared on to the end, his voice a lethal jet of flame shooting through the auditorium. He was writhing, possessed, terrible in his murderous resolution, as he ripped his crucifix off his neck and dashed it to the ground. Crouched at last like a panther, the Moor bowed again to his former gods of bloody revenge and human sacrifice.

CONCLUSION

14

Doctor Johnson on *King Lear*

Many of the foregoing opinions are personal, so let the final word on dramatic construction rest with the modern world's most formidable critic on what is arguably the world's greatest play:

The tragedy of *Lear* is deservedly celebrated among the dramas of Shakespeare. There is perhaps no play which keeps the attention so strongly fixed; which so agitates our passions and interests our curiosity. The artful involutions of distinct interests, the striking opposition of contrary characters, the sudden changes of fortune, and the quick succession of events, fill the mind with a perpetual tumult of indignation, pity, and hope. There is no scene which does not contribute to the aggravation of the distress or the conduct of the action, and scarce a line which does not conduce to the progress of the scene. So powerful is the current of the poet's imagination, that the mind, which once ventures within it, is hurried irresistibly along.

BIBLIOGRAPHY

Books on Play Construction

Dramatic Technique by George Pierce Baker. Greenwood Press.

Play-Making by William Archer. Dover Publications, New York.

The Craftsmanship of the One-Act Play by Percival Wilde. The Writer, Incorporated. Boston, USA. Covers the principles behind drama generally, not just the short play.

The Life of the Drama by Eric Bentley. Methuen. Although not designed as such, it contains much valuable comment on play construction.

An Anatomy of Drama by Martin Esslin. Published by Maurice Temple Smith. Also, an Abacus paperback.

Pinter—A study of his plays, by Martin Esslin. Chapter Four (on Pinter's dialogue.) Published by Eyre Methuen.

Dramatic Construction: An Outline of Basic Principles by Edward Mabley. Chilton Book Company, Philadelphia and New York. A technical analysis of twenty-four outstanding plays (catholic range— Sophocles to Beckett).

Aristotle's Theory of Poetry and Fine Art: translated, and with perceptive critical notes, by S. H. Butcher. Introduction by John Gassner. Dover Publications, New York.

Technique of the Drama by Gustav Freytag. Johnson Reprint Corporation, New York and London. Worth studying in conjunction with the second chapter of Bradley's *Shakespearean Tragedy*.

How Not to Write a Play by Walter Kerr. The Writer Inc., Boston, USA. Anti-Ibsen and Chekhov but pro-Shakespeare and the importance of good plotting in drama.

Harley Granville Barker: *Prefaces to Shakespeare*. Batsford. *Hamlet*; *King Lear*; *Othello*; *Coriolanus.* The sections relating to the structure and action of these tragedies.

Hitchcock: Conversations with François Truffaut. Paladin Books. Reveals many of Hitchcock's suspense techniques.

Eisenstein: *The Film Sense*. Faber. Basic work on film-making.

Nikolai Gorchakov: *Stanislavsky Directs*. More useful than Stanislavsky's own theories. We see him in action.

Understanding Drama. Cleanth Brooks and Robert Heilman. Harrap. Analyzes in detail the work of Wilde, Sheridan, Congreve, etc.

Hamburg Dramaturgy by Lessing. Dover Publications, New York. The second classic text on drama, after Aristotle.

Write That Play by Kenneth Rowe. Minerva Press, USA. Contains a line-by-line analysis of *A Doll's House* from the viewpoint of construction.

Papers on Playmaking edited by Brander Matthews. A Dramabook. Hill and Wang, New York. The comments of many playwrights on play construction.

The 36 Dramatic Situations by Georges Polti. The Writer Inc., Boston, USA. A standard work on plotting.

From Ibsen's Workshop. Edited by William Archer. Contains Ibsen's first drafts and scenarios. Da Capo Press, New York.

Arthur Miller's introduction to the collected edition of his own plays. Secker and Warburg.

Coleridge on *The Tempest* (in the Penguin edition of Coleridge's Shakespearean criticism).

Congreve's essay *Concerning Humour in Comedy.*

Act One: the autobiography of Moss Hart. Secker & Warburg.

Good theatre criticism—current or past—usually offers valuable comment on play construction. Outstanding collected volumes include:

Shaw: *Our Theatres in the Nineties*—three volumes. (Constable).

Beerbohm: *Around Theatres* and *More Theatres*. (Rupert Hart-Davis).

Kenneth Tynan: *Curtains* and *Tynan Right and Left*. (Longman).

Sheridan's play *The Critic* is a brilliant satire on playwrights, the theater profession, and the technique of play construction.

INDEX

Radio and Television

Films

Novels and Short Stories